THE GREAT LIVING TREE TIBETAN GRAMMARS

BEGINNER'S LEVEL TIBETAN GRAMMAR TEXTS BY YANGCHEN DRUBPAY DORJE

TONY DUFF

PADMA KARPO TRANSLATION COMMITTEE

First edition, August 2009
Second edition, December 2018
ISBN: paper book 978-9937-572-32-3
ISBN E-book: 978-9937-572-31-6

Janson typeface with diacritical marks and
Tibetan Classic Chogyal typeface
Designed and created by Tony Duff

Produced, Printed, and Published by
Padma Karpo Translation Committee
Ely, Minnesota 55731
U.S.A.

Committee members for this book: translation and composition, Tony Duff; editorial assistance, Sandy Hinzelin; cover design, Christopher Duff.

Web-site and e-mail contact through:
http://www.pktc.org/pktc
https://www.pktcshop.com
or search Padma Karpo Translation Committee on the web.

CONTENTS

INTRODUCTION v

1. The native texts of Tibetan grammar v
2. The need to study Tibetan grammar using native texts vi
3. A set of books to fulfil that need x
4. Thumi's treatises that define Tibetan grammar ... xiv
5. The commentaries used today to explain the treatises xvi
   a. Beginner's level: The *Great Living Tree* Tibetan grammars xxii
   b. Medium to advanced level: *Situ's Words* and *Essence of the Elegant Explanation* xxv
   c. Advanced level dealing exclusively with *The Application of Gender Signs: A Mirror that Reveals Difficult Points* and its Commentary xxviii
6. About the *Great Living Tree* grammars presented in this book xxix
7. Sanskrit xxx

"The Great Living Tree", The Essence of Thonmi's Fine Explanation *The Thirty* by Yangchen Drubpay Dorje 1

"The Fine Explanation Great Living Tree", The Clarifier of the Meaning of *The Essence of "The Thirty"* by Yangchen Drubpay Dorje 7

"The Guidance-Giving Great Living Tree", A Guide to Yangchen Drubpay Dorje's *Great Living Tree* Texts by Tony Duff 29

Glossary of Terms 53

Supports for Study 71

Tibetan Texts

The Great Living Tree 79

The Fine Explanation Great Living Tree 82

Index 95

INTRODUCTION

1. The Native Texts of Tibetan Grammar

According to Tibetan history, Thumi Saṃbhoṭa[1] defined the grammar of Tibetan language early in the 7th century C.E. in a series of eight very compact treatises. In the centuries after that until now, a number of scholars in Tibet have written commentaries to explain the meaning of the treatises. For Tibetan culture, these two types of texts—the defining treatises and the commentaries on them—are the fundamental texts through which Tibetan grammar is correctly known.

Basic Tibetan grammar is not too difficult to learn. However, to master all of it, including what are known as "the difficult points" of the grammar, is difficult. And for someone to master all of it to the point that he could write an authentic commentary on Thumi's defining treatises is very difficult. Thus, despite the fourteen centuries that have elapsed from Thumi's time until

[1] Thumi Saṃbhoṭa had several names, including the "Thonmi Saṃbhoṭa" that has become popular in recent times. Thumi is his actual name; Thonmi refers to his village.

now, there have not been many commentaries written to explain his defining treatises. And then, of the ones that have been written, only a few have gained sufficient respect that they have achieved widespread use as fundamental texts for studying grammar.

The commentaries which are most widely used for the study of Tibetan grammar today were written in the eighteenth and nineteenth centuries C.E. during a time of renaissance in learning and practice in Tibet. To begin with, the eighth Situ of the Karma Kagyu lineage of Tibetan Buddhism, a man of extraordinary learning and realization, wrote a grand commentary on grammar that re-vitalized the understanding of grammar throughout Tibet. Following that, other authors wrote a number of commentaries which agreed with and re-stated the understanding expressed in Situ's commentary, notably the Gelugpa masters Ngulchu Dharmabhadra and Yangchen Drubpay Dorje.

2. The Need to Study Tibetan Grammar Using Native Texts

When studying the grammar of a country's language, it is usual to rely on the grammar texts of that language. Therefore, it is reasonable to expect that the fundamental texts of Tibetan grammar outlined above would be the basis that non-Tibetans would use in studying the grammar of Tibetan language. However, and rather strangely, that has not been the case. Instead, some westerners have written books—primarily in English, French, and German languages—according to their idea of Tibetan grammar and these have become the books used for the purpose, even though their books do not follow Tibetan grammar as it is understood by Tibetans, but versions that only approximate it at best.

One of the biggest problems with these books is that what they present as Tibetan grammar is not actual Tibetan grammar as understood by Tibetans but a version of it which has been developed empirically. That is to say, the western authors involved have learned Tibetan grammar by observing Tibetan texts and deducing from that what the rules of Tibetan grammar must be. I was there when that approach first appeared in the early 1970's when Tibetan Buddhism and Tibetan language were first coming to the West. Almost no references to the language were in print and our knowledge of the Tibetan language was not sufficient to understand Tibetan grammar texts, so we had little choice but to take this empirical approach to understanding the grammar. However, these empirically-derived books about Tibetan grammar are now outmoded and really must be rejected as unsuited to the task. The time has arrived when we should learn the details of Tibetan grammar as it actually is and should be using the native texts of Tibetan grammar to do that.

Another major problem is that some of these books by westerners loudly proclaim systems for understanding Tibetan grammar which have no relationship at all to the systems of native Tibetan grammar. An outstanding example is the "science of the dots", which is loudly proclaimed in a major publication from western university-based scholars called as the basis for parsing and hence understanding written Tibetan language. The principal author, a friend of mine, defended his work to me by saying that his approach was found to be helpful in teaching Tibetan grammar to American students. I drily replied that his complicated system, which has nothing at all to do with native Tibetan grammar, has held back students because of filling their heads with strange ideas about it. In fact, I have found that teaching students the actual system of parsing Tibetan text as it appears in Tibetan grammar is easier than teaching them his invented system and certainly allows them to understand Tibetan language more quickly. This is not speculation; I have seen it to be so in grammar classes I have taught where I have had to patiently undo the strange system of the "science of the dots" that the students had learned from the book mentioned just above. Once the students were taught the fundamentals of the native grammar of Tibet and how they are to be applied to the process of parsing Tibetan text, they were relieved and reported that knowing the actual Tibetan system of grammar was vastly superior to knowing the system of the dots and other such inventions. I have also found that students who learned the various empirically-derived understandings of Tibetan grammar referred to above are relieved when they find out how Tibetan grammar actually works and universally report that their ability to understand the language has improved by leaps and bounds.

In spite of the fact that these books do not represent and more often than not mis-represent Tibetan grammar, they have become the basis for teaching Tibetan language and its grammar around the world: in the study programs for foreigners given at Tibetan Buddhist monasteries and the like in Nepal, India, and so on; in western university degree courses; in western Dharma centres where Tibetan language is taught; and so on. Because of them the basics of Tibetan language and its grammar have almost universally been mis-taught and mis-learned amongst non-Tibetans. Especially, their use has resulted in western translators of Tibetan Buddhism who do not really understand the grammar of the Tibetan language and whose translations suffer as a result.

As an example of this problem, some years ago Bengchen Tenga Rinpoche gave his annual course for westerners at his monastery in Nepal. He taught a text on Mahamudra that presented Mahamudra in a series of verses that were brilliantly composed with the very clever use of Tibetan grammar. Tenga Rinpoche's translator simply could not translate the material because he only knew Tibetan grammar from these empirically-derived works on Tibetan grammar that have been written by westerners. The translator was simply at a loss. His oral translation did not present the meaning of the text and teaching that went with it and, after the week of teaching had ended, none of the students got any of the meaning that Tenga Rinpoche was trying to get across to them. The teaching failed not because of the teacher, but because of a translator who simply did not understand Tibetan grammar as Tibetans understand it. Afterwards, I translated some of the text for some students who had stayed on in Nepal for a while. They were astounded at what they had missed out on. Such a sad story! Unfortunately, I have many others like it.

It is universally understood in the general world of translating and interpreting that a person who is going to translate matters of importance into another language first needs a good and correct understanding of his own language and then needs the same for the target language. In my own, direct experience, far too many people who call themselves Tibetan translators do not even know the grammar of their own language, let alone that of Tibetan. A significant factor in their not fully understanding Tibetan grammar is the books and teaching systems mentioned above that present a modified version of what Tibetan grammar actually is.

All in all, there is an outstanding need for books in languages other than Tibetan which show Tibetan grammar as it actually is. There is also an outstanding need to realize that the translation of Tibetan texts has to be based on a proper understanding of their grammar as defined in native Tibetan grammar texts.

3. A Set of Books to Fulfil that Need

In order to fulfil this need for Tibetan grammar texts that could be used as a basis for studying Tibetan grammar on its own terms, I undertook the major work of making a set of publications that would include Thumi's defining treatises and a number of respected commentaries to them, together with the explanations that would, for the first time, present Tibetan grammar to non-Tibetans in an authentic way. My aspiration for the work was that the books in general would have a very positive effect on the work of translating Tibetan Buddhist texts into other languages and in particular would result in a much higher level of quality and accuracy in the translations.

To do this work, I first had to became familiar with Thumi's defining treatises and also with the various commentaries to them, both old and new. I accomplished this through intensive studies done in the 1990's in India and Nepal with the most highly regarded Tibetan grammarians of the time. It is noteworthy that I did these studies in purely Tibetan environments, with no special arrangement made for non-Tibetans. My spoken Tibetan was already very good from years of living with Tibetans and doing oral translation for various Tibetan teachers, and I used this to advantage, learning the grammar entirely from Tibetans in Tibetan language in a purely Tibetan environment. My studies included a three month course of explanations of the entire great commentary by the eighth Situ given at the Tibetan Institute for Higher Studies in Sarnath, northern India.

In light of the knowledge of Tibetan grammatical literature gained during those studies, it seemed that the best commentaries to make available would be the ones most highly regarded and hence most used amongst Tibetans nowadays, that is, the commentaries which express Tibetan grammar as the eighth Situ explained it. My principal grammar teacher, the late Padma Gyaltsen of the Tibetan Institute of Higher Studies—who was regarded as the very best of Tibetan grammarians of his time and who certainly knew the details of the entire range of grammar commentaries that had ever been written in Tibet—agreed.

Therefore, I worked for several years on a set of books that would present the most important native Tibetan grammar texts in translation and, moreover, with all the background, glossaries, vocabulary, and so on needed to make the grammar of Tibet as Tibetans understand it not only readily comprehensible by Westerners but useful to them in a practical way.

Briefly stated, the set of books consists of two standard references to Tibetan grammar—one for each of the two extant treatises of Thumi Saṃbhoṭa—and four books each containing a specific commentary to those treatises, with the commentaries being the most popular ones in use today, commentaries which follow Situ's great commentary.[2]

---

[2] These titles are available through the PKTC web-site and shop, whose internet addresses are given on the copyright page.

The two standard references explain every detail of the grammar in a gradual way that allows beginners and scholars alike complete access to the grammar. Unlike most Western books on Tibetan grammar, the explanations included present Tibetan grammar as Tibetans understand it, though they are written so that any Westerner can easily understand them.

The first standard reference deals with history, lineages of grammar, and all the other background information needed to have a good feel for Tibetan grammar. It continues with a long presentation of the meaning of the primary text that defines Tibetan grammar, Thumi Saṃbhoṭa's treatise called *The Root of Grammar, The Thirty Verses*. This standard reference as I have called it is a very large work, containing an enormous level of detail of all relevant aspects of Tibetan grammar, and with very extensive yet easy-to-comprehend explanations of these points of grammar that show the actual Tibetan grammar in a way that works for Western minds. Step by step the explanations build a complete picture of the language and, as they do so, of all the grammar terminology involved. The standard reference faithfully presents Tibetan grammar as Tibetans understand it and as it must be understood by anyone involved with Tibetan translation. However, it includes extensive explanations which make that Tibetan understanding both comprehensible and immediately useful to Westerners because it allows them to connect that understanding with English grammar at least.

The second standard reference is written in the same detailed yet immediately useful way as the first volume. However, it deals with the subject matter of the other, remaining treatise on Tibetan grammar called *The Application of Gender Signs*. This standard reference is shorter than the first because it does not contain the extensive presentation of background material found in the first volume and because the subject matter of the second volume can be dealt with in fewer words, even though it is technically much more difficult. It is noteworthy that it includes the first complete and correct treatment of the theory of verbs and transitive-intransitive verbal actions seen in English, a topic which has confused most people because of its complexity and the absence of proper, Tibetan-grammar-based explanations of it.

The commentaries selected as supports for the explanations of the defining treatises in the two standard references to Tibetan grammar follow the eighth Situ's commentaries. They are:

- The two *Great Living Tree* grammars by Yangchen Drub pay Dorje which are the subject of this book;
- *Situ's Words* by Ngulchu Dharmabhadra;
- *The Essence of the Elegant Thorough Explanation* by Khenpo Ngedon Jamyang;
- Two commentaries to *The Application of Gender Signs* by Yangchen Drubpay Dorje.

The first standard reference also has a long chapter on pronunciation, revealing details of correct Tibetan pronunciation that still have not been seen in English. To go with that, there is a text on pronunciation by Sonam Tsemo, an early master of the Sakya tradition.

This introduction goes on to expand on the information given just above. First it gives information on Thumi's defining treatises, then on each of the commentarial texts, and finally still more information on the *Great Living Tree* grammars by Yangchen Drubpay Dorje which are the subject of this book. If you would like to see even more detailed information on all of this, together with extensive presentations of the history and lineages of Tibetan grammar, please read the first standard reference mentioned just above.

4. Thumi's Treatises that Define Tibetan Grammar

In the seventh century C.E., the Tibetan man Thumi Sambhota wrote eight treatises[3] which defined the lettering set and grammar for Tibetan language. They are the original treatises defining the Tibetan language. The first and sixth ones are still available to us but the remaining six were lost totally and irretrievably during the ninth century C.E. purges of King Langdarma. Despite many efforts since that time by great scholars of Tibet and other countries, too, no trace of them has been found.

The first treatise of Thumi is titled *The Root of Grammar, "The Thirty (Verses)"*[4]. This is usually abbreviated in Tibetan to སུམ་ཅུ་པ་ or even just སུམ་ both meaning *The Thirty*[5]. The treatise is the beginning of Thumi's definition of the Tibetan language.

---

[3] Thumi referred to them as treatises (śhāstras) because that is the Indian name for a treatise that establishes or maintains a system of thought.

[4] Tib. ལུང་སྟོན་པ་རྩ་བ་སུམ་ཅུ་པ་ཞེས་བྱ་བ་, lung ston pa rtsa ba sum cu pa zhes bya ba. Tibetan, as with English has a set of irregular spellings of numbers as one proceeds through increasingly higher numerals and the spelling of སུམ་ཅུ་ for thirty is correct.

[5] Since the number thirty refers to the number of four line verses in it, the name is often translated as *The Thirty Verses* but Thumi did not add the word for verses to the title, he simply called it *The Thirty*.

Accordingly, the main part starts with a definition of the lettering set. It then defines those letters to be of three main types when building words—prefixes, name-bases, and suffixes. The rest of it then shows how the suffix letters are used to build the necessary linking elements of the language. In doing so, it mentions many other points of Tibetan grammar by name but does not define or discuss their implications. It concludes with important definitions and advice, including how to learn and use the new grammar. Overall it makes the point that knowing the suffixes and the phrase linkers is key to understanding and being proficient with the language.

The sixth treatise has the title *Grammar, The Application of Gender Signs*. The name is usually abbreviated to *Application of Gender Signs*[6] or just *Gender Signs*[7]. It would be easy to mistake this as meaning "Grammar, the entrance or guide to signs". However, Situ Chokyi Jungney and other great grammarians point out that the meaning of « འཇུག་པ་, 'jug pa » in the title is "application of" rather than "entrance to" or "guide to".

Briefly stated, *Application of Gender Signs* defines a system of gender for the letters of the Tibetan alphabet and shows how the system is applied to the language. The application of the defined system of gender signs has a number of effects. First, there is a system of verb tenses and transitive-intransitive verb forms that happens in relation to the gender of each letter. Then, the pronunciation of each letter is defined in relation to its gender. Then, the gender of the suffix letters affects their connection to subsequent words. And so on. Like *The Thirty*, the presentation

---

[6] Tib. རྟགས་ཀྱི་འཇུག་པ་, rtags kyi 'jug pa.

[7] Tib. རྟགས་, rtags.

of the body of the text is made via the three main types of letters—prefixes, name-bases, and suffixes—and, also like *The Thirty*, the emphasis is on the fact that the suffixes are key to understanding the language.

5. The Commentaries used Today to Explain Thumi's Treatises

Ever since the ninth century, the treatises of Thumi have formed the basis of explanations of Tibetan grammar. Learned Tibetans have written texts that explained grammar according to their understanding of Thumi's work by explaining their understanding of the meaning of the two existing treatises. However, there were places in Thumi's two treatises where the meaning could be interpreted in varying ways and, on top of that, six of his treatises that contained the definitions of Tibetan grammar were missing, so differences of opinion arose in Tibet over the meaning of various matters of grammar. Thus, there came to be masters who espoused differing views of grammar. They in turn had followers who maintained the views of that master with the result that a number of lineages of Tibetan grammar arose in Tibet during the many centuries following Thumi Saṃbhoṭa's original definition of the grammar.[8]

As the centuries went by in Tibet, there were periods of rise and fall of scholarship. With that, a number of individuals who became important as Tibetan grammarians appeared at the times

---

[8] For a complete listing of the various grammarians who arose in Tibet and explanation of their grammar lineages, see volume one of the standard references to Tibetan grammar mentioned earlier in the introduction.

when scholarship was full of vitality. Of them, the ones whose works and opinions are most popular in our current time appeared in a period of renaissance which began in the 1700's.

The eighth Situ Rinpoche, Situ Chokyi Jungney, was born in Eastern Tibet in the late 1700's. He was a remarkable scholar and a very highly accomplished master of the Karma Kagyu tradition of Tibetan Buddhism. He was a central figure in the renaissance of learning that happened in Tibet during his time, writing prolifically on many subjects in both the inner and outer topics of knowledge. His works on grammar set a new standard in the understanding of grammar and his standard is the one in common use today. His writings and teachings on grammar have earned him the position of one, if not the greatest, of Tibetan grammarians.

In order to master grammar, Situ Rinpoche descended from Tibet to Nepal to learn Sanskrit properly. This might sound like the obvious thing to do for someone wanting to be an expert on Indian grammar, but it is unusual because few Tibetans actually did such a thing, it being a life-threatening proposition (for example, read Marpa Lotsawa's biography, *The Life of Marpa*). After mastering Sanskrit, Situ Rinpoche returned to Tibet and eventually wrote a large commentary on Tibetan grammar named *A Beautiful String of Pearls to Adorn the Necks of the Wise, A Thorough Explanation of the Specific Texts "The Thirty" and "Application of Gender Signs" of the Śhāstras that Authentically Set Forth the Signs of the Snowy Land*. This commentary is the centrepiece of his writings on grammar and is usually referred to as *A Beautiful String of Pearls* or more commonly as *Situ's Great Commentary*[9].

Situ's Great Commentary is an extremely difficult text to follow. There are two reasons for that. Firstly, Situ Rinpoche had a good command of Sanskrit and wrote directly about both Sanskrit and Tibetan grammars throughout his commentary. To understand the commentary, one has to understand both Sanskrit and Tibetan grammar and understand them well. Secondly, his text not only incorporates his view regarding what is correct Tibetan grammar but also puts forth all the necessary arguments to defeat whatever contrary views other grammarians might have put forth. In doing so, he quotes widely from the works of various Tibetan grammarians preceding him so, to follow the text, one has to have a considerable knowledge of the various Tibetan grammatical traditions.

The arguments about grammar amongst Tibetan scholars are mostly founded in differences of opinion that grew up because of the loss of most of Thumi's original treatises, the terseness of Thumi's extant treatises, and the lack of supporting materials from his time. An example of a major point of contention is the debate over how the vowels are defined. Thumi's definition of vowels and consonants refers to the Sanskrit system of vowels and consonants but defines them very differently and only very briefly. Most Western students of Tibetan language these days trot out with complete confidence the formulation that the Tibetan language has five vowels. Amazingly, they do so without even knowing that most Tibetans say there are four because Thumi mentions in his terse definition that there are only four marks for

[9] Tib. སི་ཏུའི་འགྲེལ་ཆེན་, si tu'i 'grel chen.

writing the vowels. Some Western students say that "Tibetan has five vowels, one of them hidden" without realizing that this is a mistaken rehash of Situ Rinpoche's final assessment of the matter and without knowing that many other grammarians disagreed with what Situ did say about it. Situ made many very cogent arguments regarding this and many other matters in his *Great Commentary*. The force of his arguments were so convincing that his system still prevails.

In short, Situ's *Great Commentary* served to give Tibetan grammar a footing that it had lost. The commentary quickly became a key piece of Tibetan literature that caused a revolution of understanding. A new lineage of Tibetan grammar developed from the explanations contained in it.

After Situ had completed his work, there were a few people who argued against it but, having read their works, it seems to me that they were just complaining for political reasons and not because of any substantial argument that they could level against Situ's words. Situ's presentation quickly became the one that was generally followed in Tibet and has stayed that way until the present because of the excellence of the explanations contained in it.[10]

---

[10] Because Situ Rinpoche's *Great Commentary* is considered by many Tibetans to be the ultimate commentary on Tibetan grammar, many Westerners have been wanting to see a translation of it. However, such a thing is very difficult to do. There are very few Tibetans who understand it properly, let alone Westerners. Allow me to say at this point that the current Situ Rinpoche personally asked me to translate this work, offering me all assistance needed and stating that he was very confident that I did have the knowledge needed to do so. His

(continued ...)

During the time of Situ, a very great Gelugpa teacher called Ngulchu Dharmabhadra [1772–1851] made a point of writing several grammar texts. Like Situ Chokyi Jungney, he was deeply concerned at the lack of understanding of grammar that prevailed in his time. He found Situ's explanations to be excellent, so he

---

[10] (... continued)
confidence was based in part on the fact that I have received months of teaching of the entire text, all in Tibetan and in a Tibetan environment, from my own grammar teacher, Padma Gyaltsen, who was regarded at that time as the greatest living Tibetan grammarian. My assessment, with the knowledge that I do have, is that it would not be very useful to do so. Here are two reasons for that assessment.

Firstly, there is the hard fact that much of the content only makes sense in Tibetan; it simply cannot be translated as such into English. It can be explained in English but the explanation could not be a mere re-phrasing of the Tibetan text. What is needed is not a translation of the text but an explanation of it. Accordingly, I have produced major works on Tibetan grammar which do just that. They explain, step by step, all of the details involved with Tibetan grammar, and in doing so, effectively present what is contained in Situ Chokyi Jungney's exceptional work.

Secondly, there is the hard fact that much of the content of *Situ's Great Commentary* is very detailed argument which might be interesting to grammar scholars but will not be of interest to someone who wants to know Tibetan grammar as a practical matter. Moreover, much of this detailed argument can only be understood with a deep understanding of both Sanskrit and Tibetan grammars. Even if someone were interested, he would not be able to understand it simply through a translation of the text. Again a major explanation of Tibetan grammar is required and that is again, exactly what I have produced in my major works on grammar.

wrote a number of texts that presented Situ's understanding and thereby became the first major successor to Situ's views of grammar. In particular, he wrote a text that presented *Situ's Great Commentary* but with all difficult and non-essential material removed. His text, known as *Situ's Words*, presents Situ's understanding of grammar but in a very readable, useful way. He did his work so well that *Situ's Words* became and still is the most widely read text of Tibetan grammar.

Ngulchu Dharmabhadra passed his lineage to his nephew Yangchen Drubpay Dorje [1809–1884] who also wrote several texts on grammar. His texts were very clear and all of them became and still are very popular. Ngulchu Dharmabhadra's writings on grammar were all at the medium to advanced level, so he asked his nephew to write a beginner's-level grammar text that would present their understanding of grammar but be very easy to understand and learn. Yangchen Drubpay Dorje followed this instruction and produced a pair of texts that quickly became the most basic texts for learning grammar. The texts are used by all Tibetans these days as the basic texts for learning grammar.

Other, well-known presentations of grammar have been made since Thumi's time. For example, Sakya Pandita [1182–1251] and Sonam Tsemo [1142–1182] both of the Sakya tradition wrote texts on grammar and followers of the Sakya tradition will sometimes use these for their studies. Similarly, there have been a number of Gelugpa scholars who have written well-known works on grammar[11]. Nonetheless, it is Situ's presentation of

---

[11] A very extensive presentation of the history of grammar in Tibet and the various major grammarians involved can be found in volume

(continued ...)

grammar and the presentations of those who followed his way of thought, especially Ngulchu Dharmabhadra and Yangchen Drubpay Dorje, that have become the main texts used for the study of grammar in Tibetan culture. Therefore, I have emphasized their works in my writings on and translations of Tibetan grammar, thinking that their works will be of the greatest benefit to non-Tibetans who are trying to learn Tibetan grammar.

a. Beginner's Level: The *Great Living Tree* Tibetan Grammars

Thumi's defining treatises are not easy to comprehend so are not used as the text-books for the study of the language. Tibetan children begin their education by learning to write the letters and pronounce the sounds of the Tibetan vowels and consonants. They then learn to write words. To go with this, they will usually learn, by heart, an abbreviated text by Yangchen Drubpay Dorje called "*The Great Living Tree*", *The Essence of Thonmi's Fine Explanation "The Thirty"*, a text which presents the essential meaning of *The Thirty* in a manner suitable for easy memorization.

Like so many other Tibetan texts, it is well-known by its poetic sub-title *The Great Living Tree*, which taken most literally means "the living tree that stands over all others". The author's intent with the words *living tree* is that his text presents the living tradition of grammar and not merely the dead assertions of people who do not really understand the subject. Then, it is the *great*

---

[11] (... continued)
one of the standard references to Tibetan grammar mentioned earlier.

tree amongst the trees in the forest of explanation; it is the one replete with leaves of the finest explanations possible and the fruit of the most enjoyable explanations possible.

To get a full feeling for the title, you have first to understand that he was writing shortly after Situ Chokyi Jungney had done his great work of reviving grammar following a long period of scholastic darkness in Tibet. Yangchen Drubpay Dorje had Situ's lineage of explanation, a lineage that was alive and vital, and which had excellent ways of explanation; it had gone beyond the deadness of understanding coupled with poor explanations which had covered Tibet. Then it has to be understood that Yangchen Drubpay Dorje was a master poet who chose this theme as the one for use throughout his texts on grammar. All in all, the title and theme of the greatest of living trees that explain grammar is a very clever way of expressing the actual situation of his time, and not merely some nice-sounding words for the name of his text.

In short, his *The Great Living Tree* text is like the greatest of living trees in a forest, the one that stands above all others, producing a luxuriant foliage and fruit of excellent explanations of grammar.

The Great Living Tree is a beginner's text. Therefore, it presents a very clear summation of Thumi's first treatise, *The Thirty*, but does not mention the other treatise, *Application of Gender Signs*. This is appropriate. Thumi's first treatise is the basis of Tibetan grammar and needs to be studied in order to know the basics.

The Great Living Tree does have something in it that most other Tibetan grammar texts do not. Neither *The Thirty* nor almost any other Tibetan text contains a guide to the use of punctuation, so *The Great Living Tree* includes some information about the use of the two main punctuation marks, tsheg's and shad's. This again is in keeping with its being a text that provides a beginner with the basics of the language.

The Great Living Tree is a very concise text meant mainly for memorization purposes. It needs explanation to make its meaning clear. Therefore, Yangchen Drubpay Dorje wrote his own commentary to clarify it and called it "*The Fine Explanation Great Living Tree" The Clarifier of the Meaning of The Essence of "The Thirty*". This commentary, which is well-known by its short title *The Fine Explanation Great Living Tree*[12], takes the root text phrase by phrase and amplifies it to make the meaning clearer.

This pair of texts has been used ever since they were written and still are used to teach the Tibetan language system to beginning students both inside and outside Tibet. As Yangchen Drubpay Dorje says in the colophon to *The Fine Explanation Great Living Tree*:

> This *Clarifier of the Meaning of the Essence of The Thirty* was written to be an easy, condensed explanation of the root, with examples, for those new, young students whose minds could not accommodate a subtle and vast … explanation.

There is a point of grammar in understanding and translating the title correctly. The wording of the title, which can be clearly understood with a good understanding of Tibetan grammar and styles of writing, does not say "Fine Explanation of the Great Living Tree". Rather, it is worded to mean that this is not the

---

[12] Tib. ལེགས་བཤད་ལྗོན་པའི་དབང་པོ་, legs bshad ljon pa'i dbang po.

great living tree itself but another one like it, a fine explanation type of great living tree. With its fine explanation, it makes clear the meaning of the other great living tree, the one which is the essence of *The Thirty*. Thus, the correct understanding of the title is "Fine Explanation Great Living Tree".

There is also a point of learning in understanding the "Great Living Tree" part of both titles. The word « ལྗོན་པ་, ljon pa » in Tibetan means a living tree as opposed to a dead one. This detail has not been well understood amongst non-Tibetans. For example, there is a living tree in the desire god realm, Heaven of the Thirty Three, and one in Amitabha's pure land, Sukhāvati. Some less knowledgeable Western translators have seen the names of these trees and assumed that the word « ལྗོན་པ་, ljon pa » used to indicate those trees must mean a heavenly tree or wish-fulfilling tree of some kind. In fact, « ལྗོན་པ་, ljon pa » simply means a living tree and it is used in the names of those two trees mentioned because the trees are alive and flourishing, no more and no less. Amazingly, this mistaken understanding has now found its way into several dictionaries! And worse, has gone from the dictionaries into further mistaken translations.

B. Medium to Advanced Level: *Situ's Words* and *Essence of the Elegant Explanation*

The most popular text for understanding grammar amongst Tibetans in general and especially amongst those following Situ's system is *The Supremely Learned Situ's Words, A Thorough Explanation of the Grammar Śhāstras of the Language of the Snowy Land, "The Thirty" and "Application of Gender Signs"* by Ngulchu

Dharmabhadra. This title is usually abbreviated to *Situ's Words*[13]. The title means that the text presents the authoritative statements spoken[14] by Situ Rinpoche regarding the two existent treatises of Thumi. *Situ's Words* is an abridgement of *Situ's Great Commentary* that leaves out all the difficult material. Ngulchu Dharmabhadra's excellent understanding of grammar allowed him to abridge the *Great Commentary* in a way that no-one else could. The work is so well done that it has become the standard text for those who want to understand grammar at the level of serious study but who cannot approach the *Great Commentary* because of its complexity and difficulty.

Then there is a grammar text that follows Situ's system but has been in use instead of *Situ's Words* as the standard text for grammar at the seat of the Karma Kagyu lineage, Tsurphu, in Tibet and now Rumtek in Sikkim. The text was written by the Kagyu khenpo called Ngedon Jamyang[15] who lived at Tshurpu in the 19th century. The full title of his commentary is *The Essence of the Elegant "Thorough Explanation", The Literal Aspect of the Snowy Land's Grammar Śhāstras, "The Thirty" and "Application of Gender Signs"*. The words in the title "*Thorough Explanation*" are an abbreviation of the full name of *Situ's Great Commentary*. The title tells exactly what the text is: a condensation of Situ's very elegantly written *Great Commentary* into an essential version of his text that gives the meaning of Thumi's treatises at the literal

[13] Tib. སི་ཏུའི་ཞལ་ལུང་, si tu'i zhal lung.

[14] Tib. ཞལ་ལུང་, zhal lung.

[15] Tib. ངེས་དོན་འཇམ་དབྱངས་, nges don 'jam dbyangs.

level[16]. The title is always abbreviated in this book to *Essence of the Elegant Explanation*.

Essence of the Elegant Explanation, like Ngulchu Dharmabhadra's *Situ's Words*, is meant to be an easier-to-understand version of *Situ's Great Commentary*. As with *Situ's Words*, it is in essence a copy of Situ's text with all of the difficult material expunged and with the author's own comments added here and there. As Khenpo Ngedon says in his preface,

> ... overall I make a commentary so that beginners can have easy access—since it touches on few difficult matters it is easy to understand. Principally though, it is the words and meanings of *A Thorough Explanation, A Beautiful Pearl Necklace* nicely condensed to their essence and arranged together with examples.

Essence of the Elegant Explanation is very similar to *Situ's Words*, nonetheless Khenpo Ngedon has his own opinion on some things and says things a little differently here and there. As well as that, the khenpo includes detail from *Situ's Great Commentary* that Ngulchu Dharmabhadra leaves out of *Situ's Words*. This makes the khenpo's commentary a useful companion to *Situ's Words*, especially for scholars.

---

[16] "Literal meaning" simply refers to the fact that this is a text written on the straightforward level of meaning and explanation. The Buddhist literary tradition distinguishes various types of explanation of a subject, such as ones that show the literal meaning, the hidden meaning, the ultimate meaning and so on, so here the author is stating which kind of explanation it is.

Texts like *Situ's Words* and *Essence of the Elegant Explanation* are the way to get into serious studies of Tibetan grammar. They provide a very realistic picture of *Situ's Great Commentary* which can be translated in a meaningful way that can be understood by non-Tibetans. I would like to suggest quite strongly to those who want to teach classes in grammar, for instance at the university level in the West or in other study institutions, that *Situ's Great Commentary* is not really very suited to the purpose but that these texts are ideal. This advice echoes the words of my own grammar teacher, Padma Gyaltsen, who said that it would be nice, he supposed, if the *Great Commentary* could be translated, but that it made much more sense to make a good, accessible translation of *Situ's Words*. He felt that *Situ's Words* was the text par excellence for studies of grammar that all but the most determined scholar would want to undertake.

c. Advanced Level Dealing Exclusively with the *Application of Gender Signs*: *A Mirror which Reveals the Difficult Points* and its Commentary

Thumi's *Application of Gender Signs* treatise is considered to be very difficult to understand and certainly not for beginners. Therefore, the beginner's level texts by Yangchen Drubpay Dorje do not deal at all with the topics contained in it. The medium to advanced texts by Ngulchu Dharmabhadra and Khenpo Ngedon Jamyang do explain the treatise and their explanations are good. However, some people want a commentary that deals exclusively with that treatise.

Such commentaries are few in number compared to the mainstream commentaries on grammar that treat both of Thumi's treatises within the one text. To find the ones which are popular today, we turn again to the uncle-nephew lineage of Zhey where we find that Ngulchu Dharmabhadra wrote commentaries that exclusively dealt with the *Application of Gender Signs* and that his nephew and student Yangchen Drubpay Dorje wrote his own texts based on them which, as with his other texts already mentioned, became very popular and have stayed that way. In particular, there is a pair of commentaries from Yangchen Drubpay Dorje that deal solely with *Application of Gender Signs*. Similar to his pair of *Great Living Tree* commentaries, the first commentary is a summary which could easily be committed to memory and the second is a long explanation of that summary. The summary text is called *A Mirror which Reveals the Difficult Points", A Short Statement of the Essential Meaning of "The Application of Gender Signs"* by Yangchen Drubpay Dorje. The commentary to that is called *A Golden Key of Knowledge, Commentary to "A Mirror that Reveals the Difficult Points of 'The Application of Gender Signs'"*. These two texts are considered to be excellent presentations of Thumi's treatise.

6. About the *Great Living Tree* Grammars Presented in this Book

The translations of the two *Great Living Tree* grammars by Yangchen Drubpay Dorje are presented in their own chapters following this introduction. Translations of Tibetan texts into another language do not always make the subject matter as clear as in the source texts simply because the original texts were intended for Tibetans living in their own environment. Therefore, I have written a new, third text in the *Great Living Tree* series called *The Guidance-Giving Great Living Tree*. It was written directly in English for non-Tibetans in order, as the name implies, to help them better understand the two *Great Living Tree*

Tibetan texts. The text appears in a chapter following the two *Great Living Tree* texts.

A glossary has been provided following the three texts in order to clarify the grammar terms found in the texts. It is usual to make a footnote in the texts at the first instance of each term that has been explained in the glossary, but we found that doing so cluttered the already complicated texts so abandoned it. Simply consult the glossary whenever you meet a technical term whose meaning needs clarification. The explanations in the glossary are brief though clear; more extensive explanations of all terms can be found in the standard references to Tibetan grammar mentioned earlier.

Finally, the Tibetan texts are presented to facilitate study.

Note that Tibetan grammar texts are not intended to be do-it-yourself books on grammar. Rather, as with most Tibetan texts, they are meant to provide a written framework for oral instruction, with the oral instruction being the real teaching on the subject.

7. Sanskrit

Sanskrit is represented in this book using the IAST system of transliteration, the system used in most academic circles. This system has been in use for many years and it is nowadays increasingly felt that it could be improved a little. In this book, the following modifications have been made to improve ease of reading and pronunciation:

ṛ is written ṛi
ḷ is written ḷi
ś is written śh
ṣ is written ṣh

ca is written as cha
cha is written as chha

Tony Duff,
Swayambunath,
Nepal,
December, 2018

"THE GREAT LIVING TREE" THE ESSENCE OF THONMI'S FINE EXPLANATION *THE THIRTY*

by Yangchen Drubpay Dorje[17]

Namo Guru Mañjughoṣhaya.

I respectfully bow to the supreme guru
Who is inseparable from Mañjughoṣha and
Having done so, will explain in a brief way
The essence of Thonmi's fine explanation, *The Thirty*.

The exhibitors of vowel function
Are the four ཨི་, ཨུ་, ཨེ་, and ཨོ་.

---

[17] The sub-title Great Living Tree « ལྗོན་པའི་དབང་པོ་, ljon pa'i dbang po » of this text is neither accidental nor mere poetry. The term « ལྗོན་པ་, ljon pa » meaning a *living tree* (and not a heavenly or magical tree as seen in some faulty dictionaries) is a deliberate choice of the author; it refers to the fact that his text is presenting the very vital grammar of the eighth Situ rather than the lifeless understanding of others prevalent at the time. Moreover, it is a *great* tree that stands above all others with its lush fruit and foliage of good explanations. The author was a master poet and came up with this theme as the way to present his books on grammar. It can be clearly seen in the titles and in the opening and closing verses of all his texts on grammar, including this one.

The consonants are the thirty of ཀ་ and so on.
ག་ང་ད་ན་བ་མ་འ་ར་ལ་ and ས་ are the ten suffixes.
ད་ and ས་ both are re-suffixes;
ད་ is obtained with ན་ར་ལ་ and
ས་ is obtained with ག་ང་བ་ and མ་.
ག་ད་བ་མ་ and འ་ are the prefixes.

གོ་ངོ་དོ་ནོ་བོ་མོ་འོ་རོ་ལོ་སོ་ and ཏོ་ are the concluders,
Also called completing words and coupled concluders.
ཏོ is connected when there is a forceful ending; འོ when there is no ending;
And the others to be concordant with the suffix at name's ending.

སུ་རུ་ར་དུ་ན་ལ་ and ཏུ་ are the seven la-equivalents;
They are used for cases two, four, and seven,
And with identity and timing.
ས་ gets སུ་; ག་བ་ and forceful ད་ get ཏུ་;
ང་ད་ན་མ་ར་ and ལ་ get དུ་;
And འ་ and no ending get ར་ and རུ་.

The five གི་ཀྱི་གྱི་འི་ and ཡི་ are the sixth case, "connective terms" and
Those five with a ས་ ending are the third case, "agentive terms".
Their mode of connection is: ན་མ་ར་ and ལ་ get གྱི་;
ད་བ་ and ས་ get ཀྱི་; ག་ and ང་ get གི་; and
འ་ and no ending get འི་ and ཡི་.

The three ཀྱང་ཡང་ and འང་ ornament and include:
ག་ད་བ་ས་ and forceful endings get ཀྱང་;

ང་ན་མ་ར་ and ལ་ endings get ཡང་; and
འ་ and no ending get འང་ and ཡང་.

The three ཏེ་དེ་སྟེ་ are continuatives:
ན་ར་ལ་ས་ and forceful endings get ཏེ་;
ད་ gets དེ་; ག་ང་བ་མ་འ་ and
No ending gets ས་ as སྟེ་.

གམ་ངམ་དམ་ནམ་བམ་མམ་འམ་
རམ་ལམ་སམ་ and ཏམ་ separate and include;
Their mode of connection is the same as concluder's case.

ར་ and རུ་; འི་ and ཡི་; འང་ and ཡང་ are distinguished
Respectively as not verse padding and padding;
འོ་ and འུ་ and འམ་ with and without
A prior tsheg are also like that.

ནས་ and ལས་ source, segregate, and include.
For actual source, either one may be connected;
Concordant-class segregation gets ནས་ and non-concordant ལས་;
For inclusion only the term ནས་ is used.

ཀྱེ་ and ཀྭ་ཡེ་ are calling terms.
They are mostly connected ahead of the names.

ནི་ is a term of segregation and of highlighting.

དང་ has the five uses of inclusion, separation, reason,
Timing, and instruction.

The དེ་ term at the beginning of a name
Has the two uses of immediately preceding convention
And accounting for something else.

ཅི་ཇི་སུ་ and གང་ are terms of generality:
ཅི་ with ཞིག་སྟེ་སླད་འདྲ་ and ཕྱིར་;
ཇི་ with སྙེད་སྲིད་ལྟར་བཞིན་ and སྐད་;
སུ་ to persons; and གང་ to all.

པ་བ་ and མ་ with and without naro are terms of the owner.
At ག་ད་ན་བ་མ་ས་ and forceful endings, པ་ is obtained.
At ང་འ་ར་ and ལ་ for terms of the owner that become far, བ་,
And for parts, the connection of པ་ is good.
པ་ and བ་ at name endings also are mostly like that.
མ་ is indefinite, connect it as required.

མ་མི་མིན་ and མེད་ are terms of negation.
མ་ and མི་ ahead, མིན་ and མེད་ at the end,
And མ་ as an in-between-consonant as well.

As for the phrase linkers ཞིང་ and so on:
ང་ན་མ་འ་ར་ལ་ endings and no ending get ཞིང་ཞེས་ཞེ་འོ་ཞེ་ན་ཞིག་;
ག་ད་བ་ and forceful ད་ endings get ཅིང་ཅེས་ཅེ་འོ་ཅེ་ན་ཅིག་;
ས་ endings, except for special ཞེས་, get ཤིང་ཤིག་ཤེ་འོ་ཤེ་ན་.
However, in ཁ་ཅིག་, ལྷན་ཅིག་, and so on,
They are part of a name so take care not to err!

When a bare letter is fronted, an ending འ་ is required;
With a hook, bend, superfix, or subfix it is dropped.

In prose where there is much meaning, at the boundary of a name;
To divide medium meanings; at completed lesser meanings;
And in verse at an ending ག, a single shad should be made.
Prose ending in a completing word and
Verse at the end of a line gets two shad.
At the completion of a great section of meaning and
At the close of a chapter, four shad are required.
Except for letter ང, there is no tsheg between a letter and a shad.

Make conscientious efforts at gaining a precise understanding of those and the rest of the topics of grammar!

This great living tree of fine explanation
Which is not obscured by a leafy-ness of words
And has fruits of meaning ripe to eat
Was propagated by Yangchen Drubpay Dorje.

❖ ❖ ❖

"THE FINE EXPLANATION GREAT LIVING TREE" THE CLARIFIER OF THE MEANING OF *THE ESSENCE OF "THE THIRTY"*[18]

by Yangchen Drubpay Dorje

OṂ SVĀSTI

The meaning in brief of *The Essence of "The Thirty"* follows.

○ Namo Guru Mañjughoṣhaya ... [19]

is Indian Sanskrit language. When translated into Tibetan it is བླ་མ་འཇམ་པའི་དབྱངས་ལ་ཕྱག་འཚལ་ལོ། and when translated into English it is "Homage to Guru Mañjughoṣha". This is the expression of worship done via Indian language.

---

[18] This text was written by the author as a commentary to the root text *The Great Living Tree*. It clarifies what is shown in it so is another great living tree, a fine explanation type of great living tree. The meaning of "great living tree" is given in the note to the title of the root text.

[19] The complexity of Tibetan root text, commentary, and English and Tibetan scripts makes it hard to pick out the various parts of the text. To assist with this, the beginning of each section of quoted root text is indicated with ○.

- I respectfully bow to the supreme guru
  Who is inseparable from Mañjughoṣha and …

is a prostration made while seeing my guru and Jetsun Mañjughoṣha inseparable in essence. This is the expression of worship done via Tibetan language.

- Having done so, will explain in a brief way
  The essence of Thonmi's fine explanation, *The Thirty*
  …

means that, of Minister Thonmi Saṃbhoṭa's two fine explanations *The Thirty* and *Gender Signs*, I will explain in a brief way the essential meaning of *The Thirty*. This is the declaration of composition.

- The exhibitors of vowel function
  Are the four ཨི་, ཨུ་, ཨེ་, and ཨོ་.
  The consonants are the thirty of ཀ་ and so on.

In general, letters are made up of both vowels and consonants. There are no letters not included within these two. Within them, our language of Snowy Tibet has for its requisites four exhibitors of the function of the āli vowels: ཨི་, ཨུ་, ཨེ་, and ཨོ་. There is also an ཨ་ "a" which is present in an un-exhibited way. The kāli consonants going from ཀ་ through ཨ་ are thirty in number.

- ག་ང་ད་ན་བ་མ་འ་ར་ལ་ and ས་ are the ten suffixes …

They are placed after the name-base, therefore they are the ten suffixes. An example of each is contained in རྟག། བཟང་། བཤད། མདུན། བཏབ། བསམ། མདའ། ཤར། དཔལ། and བྱུས།.

- ད་ and ས་ both are re-suffixes …

Both ད་ and ས་ are suffixes and not only that but, since they both get placed again after suffixes, are also re-suffixes.

- ད་ is obtained with ན་ར་ལ་ …

Re-suffix ད་ is placed with endings of the three suffixes ན་, ར་, and ལ་ as in ཕྱིནད། གྱུརད། and སྐྱལད།.

- And ས་ is obtained with ག་ང་བ་ and མ་

Re-suffix ས་ is placed with endings of ག་, ང་, བ་, and མ་ as in ཐོགས། གངས། བཏབས། and ཁམས།.

- ག་ད་བ་མ་འ་ are the prefixes …

Those letters are placed before the name-base, therefore they are the five prefixes, as in གཏོར། དཔལ། བཏབ། མཁས། and འཇམ།.

- གོ་ངོ་དོ་ནོ་བོ་མོ་འོ་རོ་ལོ་སོ་ and ཏོ་ are the concluders,
  Also called completing words and coupled concluders …

In *The Thirty* those eleven are called "concluders"; in other *Pure Letters* they are called "completing words"; and in the *Speech Door Weapon* they are called "coupled concluders". Their mode of connection is as follows.

- ཏོ་ is connected when there is a forceful ending; འོ་ when there is no ending …

When there is a forceful ད་, that is, a re-suffixed ད་, ཏོ་ is obtained as in ཕྱིནད་ཏོ། གྱུརད་ཏོ། and སྐྱལད་ཏོ།. Where there is no ending འོ་ is obtained, for example, བྱའོ།.

- And the others to be concordant with the suffix at the
  name's ending …

means that the others must be connected so that they are concordant with whatever suffix is present at the name's ending, as in སྨུག་གོ་ བཟང་ངོ། བཤད་དོ། བསན་ནོ། བཏབ་བོ། བསམ་མོ། མདའ་འོ། ཤར་རོ། གསལ་ལོ། and བྲུས་སོ།.

- སུ་རུ་ར་དུ་ན་ལ་ཏུ་ are the seven la-equivalents.

Those seven are called "the seven la-equivalent cases[20]". What meanings are they used to give?

- They are used for cases two, four, and seven,
  And with identity and timing.

They are used to give five meanings:

case two, "site of a function" as in ཤར་ཕྱོགས་སུ་འགྲོ། "went to the east";

case four, "necessity and purpose" as in རྟར་རྩྭ་བྱིན། "gave grass to the horse";

case seven, "site of support" as in ལྷ་ཁང་དུ་རྟེན་གསུམ་ཡོད། "there are three representations in the shrine-room";

the internal division of case two called "identity" as in འོད་དུ་འཚེར། "radiating light";

and the internal division of case seven called "timing" as in ཉི་མའི་འཆར་ཁ་རུ་འགྲོ། "go at sun-rise".

Their mode of connection is as follows.

---

[20] A case in Tibetan means any phrase linker that actually produces a case by its being written down and, of course, at the same time marks the case. So these are the seven la-equivalent terms that both produce and mark cases.

○ ས་ gets སུ་ …

that is, an ending ས་ gets སུ་ as in གཡས་སུ། and ལས་སུ།.

○ ག་བ་ and forceful ད་ get ཏུ་ …

that is, ག་བ་ and forceful ད་ endings get ཏུ་, for example, འགག་ཏུ། ལག་ཏུ། རྒྱབ་ཏུ། འགབ་ཏུ། ཀུནད་ཏུ། སྒྱུརད་ཏུ་གསོལ། and སྤྲུལད་ཏུ་གསོལ།.

○ ང་ད་ན་མ་ར་ and ལ་ get དུ་ …

that is, those six endings get དུ་, for example, སྟེང་དུ། བཤད་དུ། མདུན་དུ། ལམ་དུ། གསེར་དུ། and དཔལ་དུ།.

○ And འ་ and no ending gets ར་ and རུ་ …

that is, when འ་ is at the ending position or when there is no ending, ར་ or རུ་, whichever is appropriate, is obtained, as in ཧྡ་མདར། and ཧྡ་མདའ་རུ།, and in ཁར། and ཁ་རུ།.

○ The five གི་ཀྱི་གྱི་འི་ and ཡི་ are the sixth case, "connective terms" …

These without a ས་ ending are the sixth case, terms that connect preceding and succeeding phrases. In the example ཟངས་ཀྱི་ཞག་ཀླུག "a bronze butter-tea urn", the term connects concordant bases; in སྟེང་གི་མི། "the man above", the term connects support and supported; in ལག་པའི་སོར་མོ། "the hand's finger", the term connects something having limbs with its limbs; and so on.

○ And those five with a ས་ ending are the third case, "agentive terms" …

Those five terms གི་ and so on but with a ས་ ending are third cases, terms of the agent. These cases have the meaning that their recipients—the places to which they are connected—are performing an action, no matter whether the verb of the action is close to the recipient or not; for example in མིག་གིས་བལྟས། "looked with the eyes" where the verb of the action is close by the agent and in མིག་གིས་ཞལ་རྒྱེའི་རྒྱ་མོ་ནས་ཕྱོགས་ཐམས་ཅད་དུ་ཡང་དང་ཡང་དུ་ལེགས་པར་བལྟས་སོ། "looked carefully again and again in every direction through a telescope with the eyes" where the verb is far from it.

For both the sixth and the third cases the mode of connection is as follows.

- Their mode of connection is: ན་མ་ར་ and ལ་ get གྱི་ …

At those endings, the sixth and third cases get གྱི་, for example: མདུན་གྱི། "the front of" and མདུན་གྱིས་བལྟས། "looked at from the front"; གཏམ་གྱི་འོག "latter part of the story" and གཏམ་གྱིས་བཤད། "explained with a story"; ཆར་གྱི་ཐིགས་མ། "drops of rain" and ཆར་གྱིས་ཚོས། "cooked with rainwater"; ཆོས་དཔལ་གྱི་ཕྱག "Chopal's hand" and ཆོས་དཔལ་གྱིས་གསུངས། "Chopal said".

- ད་བ་ and ས་ get ཀྱི་ …

At those endings, the sixth and third cases get ཀྱི་, for example: ཁྱོད་ཀྱི་གདོང་པ། "your face" and ཁྱོད་ཀྱིས་བཤད། "you explained, explained by you"; རྒྱབ་ཀྱི་གོས། "clothing of the back" and རྒྱབ་ཀྱིས་ཁྱེར། "carried on the back (literally, carried by back)"; གོས་ཀྱི་ཆ་ག "hem of the clothing" and གོས་ཀྱིས་གཡོགས། "covered with clothing (that is, dressed, not naked)". In addition, it should be understood by implication that a forceful ད་ also gets ཀྱི་.

- ག་ and ང་ get གི་ …

At both of those endings, the sixth and the third cases get གི་, for example: བདག་གི་ནོར། "my wealth" and བདག་གིས་བཤད། "I explained, explained by me"; ཆང་གི་སྙང་མ། "the lees of the beer" and ཆང་གིས་ར་རོ། "intoxicated by beer".

- འ་ and no ending gets འི་ and ཡི་ …

When འ་ is at the ending position or there is no ending, the sixth and third get འི་ or ཡི་ whichever suits as in མདའི་ལྟོང་། and མདའ་ཡི་ལྟོང་། "notch of an arrow"; and མདས་བསད། and མདའ་ཡིས་བསད། "killed by an arrow"; ཁའི་སོ། and ཁ་ཡི་སོ། "teeth of the mouth"; and ཁས་ཟས། and ཁ་ཡིས་ཟས། "ate with the mouth".

- The three ཀྱང་ཡང་འང་ ornament and include …

When these are placed they have two meanings as phrase ornaments and a third meaning as inclusion.

Firstly, they are placed as phrase ornaments of concordance in which they show concordance between preceding and succeeding phrases, as in མཛེས་ཀྱང་མཛེས། "more beautiful than beautiful!" དྲི་མ་ཁ་ཡང་ཁ། "a thoroughly bad smell", ཤ་ཟའང་ཟ། "ate and ate meat".

Secondly, they are placed as phrase ornaments of non-concordance in which they show non-concordance of preceding and succeeding phrases, as in མཛེས་ཀྱང་གོས་མེད། "beautiful but without good clothes"; ཀུན་གྱི་ལྷ་ཡང་མཆོད་མཁན་མེད། "all the deities but no-one to make offerings"; རྒྱན་དགའང་ཕྱིས་བདར་མེད། "nice jewellery but tarnished".

Thirdly, ཀྱང་ and so on can include another item when they are placed to have that meaning, as in ལྷས་ཀྱང་བཏུད་དོ། "the gods also bowed", ཤ་ཡང་ཟ། "Eat meat, too!", and ལྕེའང་ཚིག་ "burned the tongue as well".

- ག་ད་བ་ས་ and forceful endings get ཀྱང་ …

At those endings ཀྱང་ is obtained, for example, བདག་ཀྱང་འགྲོ། "I will go too"; བཤད་ཀྱང་མི་ཉན། "explained to but not listening"; རྒྱབ་ཀྱང་ན། "back hurt, too"; ཆོས་ཀྱང་ཤེས། "also knew the dharma"; ཕྱིན་ཀྱང་མ་སླེབ། "left but not arrived yet"; བཀའ་བསྒྲུར་ཀྱང་མི་ཉན། "was ordered but did not listen to the command"; བཀའི་སྐུལད་ཀྱང་མི་གོ "was given explanations but did not understand".

- ང་ན་མ་ར་ and ལ་ endings get ཡང་ …

At those endings ཡང་ is obtained, for example, ལྷ་ཁང་ཡང་ཡོད། "there is a shrine-room, too"; ལན་ཡང་མི་འདེབས། "do not even reply"; ལམ་ཡང་ནོར། "mistook the way, too"; ཁར་ཡང་བཅུག "also put into the mouth"; དཔལ་ཡང་ཆེ། "even greater glory".

- And འ་ and no ending gets འང་ and ཡང་ …

When འ་ is at the ending position or when there is no ending, འང་ or ཡང་ whichever suits is obtained, as in མདའང་ཤེས། and མདའ་ཡང་ཤེས། "knew archery, too"; སྣའང་རིང་། སྣ་ཡང་རིང་། "also was not short-tempered".

- The three ཏེ་དེ་སྟེ་ are continuatives …

At the end of a name, a bare ཏ་ as ཏེ་ then as དེ་ then with ས་ as སྟེ་ have, in short, the meaning of leading on to something extra that is still to be shown. For example, in ཕྱག་འཚལ་ཏེ་བཤད། "prostrated then spoke"; ཆོས་བཤད་དེ་གོ "the dharma was spoken and understood"; སོང་སྟེ་སླེབས། "went then arrived".

Their mode of connection is as follows.

- ན་ར་ལ་ས་ and forceful endings get ཏེ་ …

At those six endings[21], bare ཏ་ as ཏེ་ is obtained as in ཉན་ཏེ་གོ “listen and understand”; འཕར་ཏེ་འགྲོ། “got up and left”; དགྲ་བཏུལ་ཏེ་ཡོང་། “overcame the enemies then returned”; ཇོས་ཏེ་ཚིག “cut down and burn (after the harvest); ཕྱིནད་ཏེ་བསླེབས། “left and arrived”; ཆོས་བསྒྱུར་ཏེ་བཤད། “translated and spoke the dharma”; སྤུལད་ཏེ་ཡི་རང་། “pleased and accepted what was told”.

- ད་ gets དེ་ …

At that ending, དེ་ is obtained as in བསད་དེ་ཟ། “kill and eat”.

- ག་ང་བ་མ་འ་ and no ending get ས་ as སྟེ་ …

At those six endings ས་ as སྟེ་ is obtained as in ཆུ་བཀག་སྟེ་བསྒྱིལ། “the dammed waters pooled together“; འཕང་སྟེ་འཕོག “fired and hit”; འབྲུ་བཏབ་སྟེ་སྐྱེས། “the grain was planted and grew”; དོན་བསམ་སྟེ་སྒོམ། “contemplated the meaning then cultivated it”; ལུང་པའི་མདའ་སྟོ་གུ་ཡངས།”the confluence of the valley was broad and open”; རྡོ་སྟེ་ཤིན་ཏུ་སྲ། “(like) rock; very hard”.

- གམ་ངམ་དམ་ནམ་བམ་མམ་འམ་
  རམ་ལམ་སམ་ and ཏམ་ separate and include …

These eleven of གམ་ and so on, are placed to have the meaning of separation of multiple items where they are being separated out of one basis, as in བུམ་པའི་རྒྱུ་ནི་གསེར་རམ། དངུལ་ལམ། ཟངས་སམ། རག་གམ། རྫ་ལས་བྱའོ། “The substances used to make pots are gold, silver, brass, bronze, and terracotta”. They are also placed to have the meaning of inclusion of multiple items which are being put into one basis, as in གསེར་རམ། དངུལ་ལམ། ཟངས་སམ། རག་གམ། རྫ་ལས་བུམ་པ་བྱའོ། “Gold, silver, brass, bronze, and clay are used to make pots”.

---

[21] Two forceful endings are included.

Additionally, these eleven are stated to have the meaning of separation where the distinctions "is, is not" and "exists, does not exist" are being made, as in ཡིན་ནམ་མིན། "either is or is not" and ཡོད་དམ་མེད། "either exists or does not exist".

Their mode of application is as follows.

- Their mode of connection is the same as concluder's
  case ...

"When there is a forceful ད་", ཏམ་ is obtained as in ཕྱིན་དཏམ། གྱུརད་ཏམ། སྤྲུལད་ཏམ།. "When there is no ending", འམ་ is obtained as in ཁའམ།. "And the others to be concordant with the suffix at name's ending" means that the others must be connected so that they are concordant with whatever suffix is present at the name's ending, as in སྟག་གམ། བཟང་ངམ། ཡོད་དམ། ཡིན་ནམ། ལབ་བམ། བསམ་མམ། མཐའ་འམ། ཤར་རམ། གསལ་ལམ། and བྱས་སམ།.

- ར་ and རུ་; འི་ and ཡི་; འང་ and ཡང་ are distinguished
  Respectively as not verse padding and padding.

There are the la-equivalents ར་ and རུ་, the sixth and third cases འི་ and ཡི་, and the ornament-inclusion terms འང་ and ཡང་. When a line of verse does not need padding ར་, འི་, and འང་ are obtained as in རང་ཉིད་ལྷར་གསལ་ཐུགས་ཀ་ནས། །དཔལ་ལྷའི་ཕྱག་གི་མདའ་དར་ནི། ། ལྷ་མོའང་བདག་ལ་ཞེན་ཏུ་དཀྲིས།. When a line does need padding རུ་, ཡི་, and ཡང་ are obtained as in རང་ཉིད་ལྷ་རུ་གསལ་ནས་ནི། །ལྷ་ཡི་ཕྱག་གི་མདའ་དར་ནི། ལྷ་ཡང་བདག་ལ་ཞེན་ཏུ་དཀྲིས།.

- འོ་ and འུ་ and འམ་ with and without
  A prior tsheg are also like that.

When a line of verse does not need padding, the འོ་ of concluders, the འུ་ of names, and the འམ་ of separation-inclusion do not get a tsheg before them as in དཔལ་ལྡན་ལྷ་མོའོ་སྐྱོང་མའི་གཙོ། |ཕད་མའི་ཟེའུ་འབྲུ་དག་ལས་སྐྱེས། |བདུད་མོའམ་ཡང་ན་འབའ་མོ་སྟེ།. When a line does need padding, they do get a tsheg before them as in འདི་ནི་དཔལ་ལྡན་ལྷ་མོ་འོ། |ཟེ་འུ་འབྲུ་ལ་བརྟུས་ཏེ་སྐྱེས། |ལྷ་འམ་ཡང་ན་བདུད་མོ་སྟེ།.

- ནས་ and ལས་ source, segregate, and include …

Both ནས་ and ལས་ are placed to mean the fifth case, actual source. They are also placed to mean its aspects, segregation out from a basis and inclusion of many things. The difference between them is as follows.

- For actual source, either one may be connected …

When it is actual source, it is all right to connect either ནས་ or ལས་, for example in ས་ནས་རྩྭ་སྐྱེ། and ས་ལས་རྩྭ་སྐྱེས། "grass grows from the ground" and in བ་ལས་འོ་མ་འཇོ། and བ་ནས་འོ་མ་འཇོ། "milk is obtained from cows".

In segregation there are two:

- Concordant-class segregation gets ནས་ …

When the basis from which the segregation is made and that which is segregated from it are of concordant class, only ནས་ and never ལས་ is obtained, as in ལྷ་རྣམས་ཀྱི་ནང་ནས་བརྒྱ་བྱིན་གཟུགས་མཛེས། "of the various gods, Kaushika has the most beautiful form".

- … and non-concordant ལས་.

When the basis from which the segregation is made and that which is segregated from it are of non-concordant class, only ལས་ and never ནས་ is obtained, as in ལྷ་ལས་མི་དམན། "men are lower than gods".

- For inclusion only the term ནས་ is used …

For the purpose of inclusion, the term ནས་ alone is placed, due to which ལས་ is not obtained, as for example in: སྤྱི་གཙུག་ནས་རྐང་མཐིལ་གྱི་བར། "from the top of the head to the soles of the feet".

- ཀྱེ་ and ཀྭ་ཡེ་ are calling terms …

With a distinguished object, ཀྱེ་ is placed; with an equal object ཀྭ་ཡེ; and it is shown only by implication but with an inferior object ཀས་, ཧ་ཡི་, and ཧས་ are placed.

Their mode of connection is that:

- They are mostly connected ahead of the names.

It is necessary to connect these ahead of most names of whoever is to be called, as in ཀྱེ་རྒྱལ་པོ་ཆེན་པོ། "Oh, great king!"; ཀྭ་ཡེ་གྲོགས་པོ། "Oh friend!"; ཀྭས་མ་ཆེན། "Hey, cook …"; ཧ་ཡེ་ཆེ་བ་དཔོན། "Excuse me, you there in charge of the elderly!"; ཧས་བོང་དཔོན། "Oy, you in charge of the donkeys!" However, it sometimes it must be connected at the end of the name, for example ངག་གི་དངོས་གྲུབ་སྩོལ་ཅིག་དབྱངས་ཅན་ཀྱེ། "Oh Sarasvati, grant me the siddhi of speech!"

- ནི་ is a term of segregation and of highlighting.

Placement of ནི་ is used for the two meanings of segregation out from a basis of segregation and highlighting. As an example of the first, segregation, སྔོན་འགྲོ། དངོས་གཞི། མཇུག་གསུམ་ལས་དང་པོ་སྔོན་འགྲོ་ནི། "of the three, the preliminaries, main part, and conclusion, the preliminaries for a beginner are:". And as an example of the second, highlighting, ཇ་ནི་བྱུང་། མར་ནི་བྱུང་། ཚྭ་ནི་བྱུང་། བུལ་ནི་བྱུང་། "Tea—got that; butter—got that; salt—got that;

ladle—got that. In wordings like སྨོམ་པ་ཐམས་ཅད་ལྡན་པར་ནི། padding words also become a term that highlights.

- ངང་ has the five uses of inclusion, separation, reason,
  Timing, and instruction.

The so-called "ངང་ dang which sits in between words" is placed to give these five meanings:

inclusion into a basis of separation at the end, as in མིག་དང་། རྣ་བ་དང་། སྣ་དང་། ལྕེ་དང་། ལུས་རྣམས་ནི་དབང་པོའོ། "eyes, ears, nose, tongue, and body are sense faculties";

separation out from a basis of separation present at the beginning, as in དབང་པོ་ལྔ་ནི་མིག་དང་། རྣ་བ་དང་། སྣ་དང་། ལྕེ་དང་། ལུས་པོ། "the five sense faculties of eyes, ears, nose, tongue, and body";

a reason, as in ཡི་གེ་བྲིས་པ་དང་དག་བྱེད་མཁས་མིན་ཤེས་སོ། "he wrote letters so we knew that he was not good at grammar";

timings that express time, as in ཉི་མ་ཤར་བ་དང་འགྲོ། "we go with the sunrise";

giving a verbal instruction, as in ཡི་གེ་བྲིས་དང་། སུམ་རྟགས་སྦྱོང་དང་། དག་ཡིག་ཟིན་དང་། "learn to write, study *The Thirty* and *Gender Signs*, and memorize *Pure Letters*."

- The དེ term at the beginning of a name
  Has the two uses of immediately preceding convention
  And accounting for something else.

The དེ་ term present at the beginning of a name is explained as having many usages with different meanings. However, to summarize them, it is used for both the preceding convention and accounting for something else. It is placed:

1. with just that immediately preceding thing in the flow of expression, as in མི་གཞོན་པའོ། །དེ་གཟུགས་རིང་ངོ་། ། དེ་ངོ་ཞིང་ཆེའོ། །དེ་སྐད་སྟོམ་མོ། "The man is young. He is tall. His face is broad. His voice is deep";
2. to account for something else which is the use of the དེ་ term to stand in for something else which needs to be accounted for even though it is not obvious, as in: དེ་ལ་ལྟོས་ཤིག "Rely on that!", དེ་མ་ཤོད་ཅིག "Don't speak of that!" དེ་ཁྱེར་ཤོག "Please carry it!"

- ཅི་ཇི་སུ་ and གང་ are terms of generality

Those four, ཅི་ and so on, are placed to give the meaning of encompassing generalities, the non-specifics.

Their mode of connection is as follows:

- ཅི་ with ཞིག་སྟེ་སྐད་འདྲ་ and ཕྱིར་ …

ཅི་ is used with the five, ཞིག་ and the others, as in ཅི་ཞིག ཅི་སྟེ། ཅི་སྐད། ཅི་འདྲ། and ཅིའི་ཕྱིར།. And it is also workable to connect ཞིག་ to ཇི་, as for example with ཇི་ཞིག་.

- ཇི་ with སྙེད་སྲིད་ལྟར་བཞིན་ and སྐད་ …

ཇི་ is applied to the five, སྙེད་ and the others, as in ཇི་སྙེད། ཇི་སྲིད། ཇི་ལྟར། ཇི་བཞིན། and ཇི་སྐད།.

- སུ་ to persons …

སུ་ is used with sentient persons as in སུ་ཡིན། སུ་ཡིས་ཟེར། and སུ་ལ་ཡོད།.

- And གང་ to all.

གང་ is used with everything, both that which has a mind and that which does not have a mind, as in གང་ནས་ཡིན། and གང་ཞིག་ཡིན།.

- པ་བ་མ་ with and without naro are terms of the owner …

There are the three items པོ་, བོ་, and མོ་ with a naro and the three items པ་, བ་, and མ་ without a naro. When those six are connected for the first time to a word that previously did not have such a part—such as རྡོལ་ཡས། གྱོལ། ཕྱུག འགག ལྷ་རྗེ། and ཚང་།—they are like the owner of or thing present with the name which now shows a meaning that did not show previously. This is the term of the owner, for example in རྡོལ་ཡས་པོ། གྱོལ་པོ། ཕྱུག་མོ། འགག་པ། ལྷ་རྗེ་བ། and ཚང་མ།.

Their mode of connection is as follows.

- At ག་ད་ན་བ་མ་ས་ and forceful endings, པ་ is obtained …

At those endings the term of the owner པ་ is obtained as in གཡག་པ། བཞད་པ། ལྡན་པ། ལབ་པ། གྲོང་གསུམ་པ། དབུས་པ། ཕར་ཕྱིནད་པ། དབང་བསྒྱུརད་པ། and ཆུ་བསྐྱིལད་པ།.

- At ང་འ་ར་ and ལ་ for terms of the owner that become far, བ་ …

When names with one of those five endings have no place of addition, the term of the owner becomes something else added farther along in which case the connection of the half བ་ which is a ཝ་, as in ཁ་བྱང་བ། རྟ་མདའ་བ། བྱང་ཤར་བ། ཁམས་རྡོལ་བ། and གཞིས་རྩེ་བ། is good.

- And for parts, the connection of པ་ is good …

When names have a place of addition, the term of the owner becomes part of the name, in which case the connection of པ་ for the most part is good, as in བྱང་པ། མདའ་པ། གུར་པ། རྡོལ་པ། and རྩེ་པ།.

- པ་ and བ་ as name-endings also are mostly like that.

The པ་ and བ་ at the end of a name which are not a term of the owner also have a mode of connection which for the most part is like that, as in ལག་པ། and རྐང་པ།.

- མ་ is indefinite, connect it on circumstance.

As for the མ་ term of the owner, what gets it is not definite, therefore it is connected as required, as in ཛ་མ། ཚང་མ། ཐང་མ། and རོང་མ།.

- མ་མི་མིན་ and མེད་ are terms of negation …

When those four are connected to something, they are terms of negation, showing that the meaning of the recipient to which they have been connected is "is not" or "does not exist".

Their mode of connection is as follows.

- མ་ and མི་ ahead …

The two terms of negation མ་ and མི་ must be connected ahead of that to be negated, as in མ་ཡིན། and མི་འདུག. Then,

- མིན་ and མེད་ at the end …

The two terms of negation མིན་ and མེད་ must be connected at the end of that to be negated, as in ལྷ་མིན། and འདྲེ་མེད།.

- And མ་ as an in-between-consonant as well.

The term of negation མ་ must be connected ahead of that to be negated but that is not its only use. It is used as an in-between-consonant as well; when connected between two items to be negated, it is able to negate the items on either side of it, as in རྟ་མ་བོང་། "neither horse nor ass" and in ར་མ་ལུག་ "neither goat nor sheep".

- As for the phrase linkers ཞིང་ and so on …

ཞིང་ and the rest, ཅིང་ and the rest, and ཤིང་ and the rest are like linkers that bring together previous and subsequent phrases. Their mode of connection is as follows.

- ང་ན་མ་འ་ར་ལ་ and no ending get ཞིང་ཞེས་ཞེ་འོ་ཞེ་ན་ཞིག་.

The five of ཞིང་ and the rest must be connected at the seven endings of ང་ and so on, for example as in སོང་ཞིང་། སོང་ཞེས་ཟེར་རོ། སོང་ཞེའོ། སོང་ཞེ་ན། ལྷ་ཁང་ཞིག་ཡོད། and similarly, but with the type of ending alternated, as in བྱོན་ཞིང་། བསམ་ཞིང་། མི་འདའ་ཞིང་། སློར་ཤར་ཞིང་། གསལ་ཞིང་། and ཞལ་ལ་ལྟ་ཞིང་།.

- ག་ད་བ་ and forceful ད་ endings get ཅིང་ཅེས་ཅེ་འོ་ཅེ་ན་ཅིག་.

The five ཅིང་ and so on must be connected where there is a ག་ད་བ་ or forceful ད་ for example as in བཀག་ཅིང་། བཀག་ཅེས་ཟེར་རོ། ། བཀག་ཅེའོ། །བཀག་ཅེ་ན། རྒྱུ་ཕྱོག་ཅིག and similarly, but with the type of ending alternated, as in བཤད་ཅིང་། བཀབ་ཅིང་། ཡིནད་ཅིང་། ཡི་གེ་བསྒྱུརད་ཅིང་། རྒྱུ་བསྐྱིལད་ཅིང་།.

- ས་ endings, except for special ཞེས་, get ཤིང་ཤིག་ཤེ་འོ་ཤེ་ན་.

At ས་ endings, there is the special case of having to connect the phrase linker ཞེས་ instead of ཤེས་ as in ཆོས་བྱུས་ཞེས་ཟེར་རོ།. Except for that, ས་ endings get the four of ཤིང་, ཤིག་, ཤེ་འོ་, and ཤེ་ན་ as in བྱུས་ཤིང་།, ཕྱིས་ཤིག, བྱུས་ཤེའོ།, and བྱུས་ཤེ་ན།.

The ཞེའོ་, ཅེའོ་, and ཤེའོ་ mentioned above have the meaning of ཟེར་རོ། "said" and the ཞེ་ན་, ཅེ་ན་, and ཤེ་ན་ mentioned above have the meaning of ཟེར་ན་ "if it is said, asked".

- However, in ཁ་ཅིག, ལྷན་ཅིག་, and so on,
  They are part of a name so take care not to err!

However, in ཁ་ཅིག ལྷན་ཅིག ཆབས་ཅིག ཐབས་ཅིག སྟབས་ཅིག སྐབས་ཅིག and so on, they are not a phrase linker but part of a name, so be very careful not to make an error here.

- When a bare letter is fronted, an ending འ་ is required;
  With a hook, bend, superfix or subfix it is dropped.

"Hook" means gigu or zhabkyu; "bend" means drengbu or naro; "superfix" means ra-head, la-head, or sa-head; and "subfix" means the four sub-fixes ya, ra, la, and wa.

Whatever does not have any of those at all is "bare" and whenever any of the five prefixes is fronted onto such an bare letter, an འ་ ending is definitely required, for example in དཔའ་བོ།, མདའ་པ།, and འགའ་ཞིག. For letters which do have a hook, a bend, a superfix and-or a subfix as explained above[22], the affixed འ་ must be dropped as in: སེམས་ཅན་གཡི།, གྭ་པ།, དར་བའི་བདེ།, གོ་བྱེད་བརྡ།, and རྒྱང་ཧེ་ཡུ་མོ།.

Now regarding the shad of dbu can and dbu med too, All-knowing Dharmabhadra considers that tsheg's and shad's should be placed as follows.[23]

---

[22] … and hence which are not "bare" …

[23] Thumi Saṃbhoṭa devised two main forms of lettering for the Tibetan language: one with and one without serifs on the heads of the letters called dbu can ("has heads") and dbu med ("without heads") respectively. He also devised a system of punctuation to go with these lettering sets in which the two main break marks are the vertical stroke । called a "shad" and the small mark (it is not a dot!) ་ called a "tsheg". His system for the use of these marks is not explained in either of his two remaining treatises; it is only known

(continued ...)

- In prose where there is much meaning, at the boundary of a name …

In prose where there is much meaning, a shad or tsheg-shad is not positioned where its placement would cut across a name but at the boundary of the name as in རིན་པོ་ཆེའི་ཟ་མ་ཏོག་དང་།   ངག་གི་སྒྲོལ་མ་དང་།   ཡི་ཤེའི་གུར་ཁང་སོགས་ལ།.

- To divide medium meanings …

Where there is an amount of meaning which is just middling and a shad is needed in order to separate name-equivalents, a single shad is placed at the boundary of the name as in སུམ་རྟ་པ་དང་། རྟགས་འཇུག་གི་ལྷ་བུ།.

- At completed lesser meanings …

When a lesser meaning has no more to it, a shad is positioned at each completion boundary as in དེ་རང་ཡིན་ནོ།.

- And in verse at an ending ག་, a single shad should be made.

Verse which has ག་ at the end of the line gets a single shad as in རྣམ་གྲངས་གཞན་ཅན་གཉིས་ལ་འཇུག   །…….

- Prose ending in a completing word and …

Prose that ends in one of the completing words—གོ་, ངོ་, དོ་, ནོ་, etcetera—gets two shad, for example in འདི་ནི་རྒྱུད་དོ།   །…….

---

[23] (... continued)
by oral tradition. The rules for the placement of a shad that he is about to give equally apply to both types of lettering. He only says that in relation to shad's because what he is about to say about tshegs does apply equally to both types of lettering but for dbu med lettering there are some additional considerations for their use.

- Verse at the end of a line gets two shad.

In verse, all lines that do not have ག་ at the end get two shad at the end, as for example in བླ་མ་མཆོག་དང་དབྱེར་མེད་པའི། །.......

- At the completion of a great section of meaning and …

The completion boundary of a great section of meaning gets four shad, as for example in: དག་བྱེད་གསལ་བའི་མེ་ལོང་རྫོགས་སོ།། །།ལྷ་བྲུ།.

- At the close of a chapter four shad are required.

The boundary of a ལེའུ་ chapter, gets four shad as in སྒྲ་བསྡམས་པའི་ལེའུ་སྟེ་དང་པོའོ།། །།ལྷ་བྲུ།.

- Except for letter ང་, there is no tsheg between a letter and a shad

In the case of dbu can only, a "differentiating-tsheg" or "nga-tsheg" is required between a final letter ང་ nga and a shad in order to stop the possibility of that construction being mistaken for ཏ་, as in མ་བསྒྲིབས་ཤིང་།; other letter-shad combinations do not have a tsheg inserted in between as for example in གཡུར་ཟ་བའི།.

- Make conscientious efforts at gaining a precise understanding of those and the rest of the topics of grammar

There are few words here but it is necessary to make an effort to examine and analyse them precisely. This clarifier of the meaning of *The Essence of "The Thirty"* was written to be an easy to understand, condensed explanation of the root with examples for those new, young students whose minds could not accommodate a subtle and vast explanation. Once it has been mastered, I request them please to examine and analyse precisely, over and again, texts with more examples and after that the reference works that extensively show the meaning of *The Thirty* and so to go by whatever means possible to complete expertise in the meaning of *The Thirty*.

This living tree of clarifying explanation,
The greatest of all living trees,
Not obscured by leafy-ness of un-necessary words
Dangling and swaying about
And having the supreme fruit, the necessary definitive
meaning,
Ripe and ready to eat with juice of one hundred flavours,
Came to life from the sustenance that maintains the intellect
Of Yangchen Drubpay Dorje.

Śhubam![24]

---

[24] Śhubham is a Sanskrit term often used as an ending to Tibetan texts. Sanskrit is often used by Tibetan authors at the beginning and end of a text in order to retain a connection with the Indian origin of Buddhism. The term itself mean "Prosperity!"

"THE GUIDANCE-GIVING GREAT LIVING TREE"

by Tony Duff

Yangchen Drubpay Dorje wrote his own commentary to the *Great Living Tree* text but he wrote it for the use of Tibetans in a Tibetan cultural setting which means that its meaning will not be readily apparent to people from other cultures. Therefore, I have written this short guide to the *Great Living Tree* in order to make the content more accessible for non-Tibetans. Accordingly, I have called it the *Guidance-Giving Great Living Tree*.

Note that the purpose of this guide is to make the content of the text more accessible for beginners, not to provide a full explanation of all the matters contained in the text. A full explanation requires a much longer treatment , which can be found in the standard references to Tibetan grammar mentioned in the introduction.

A very important point to understand is that, although Yangchen Drubpay Dorje's books were written for beginners, they were not written to be "teach yourself" or "do it yourself books". Rather, they were written to be a basis only for oral instruction, person to person. The style of writing is very simple, which makes them accessible to beginners but they only become fully accessible when there is a teacher. Therefore, again, this short guide to the meaning does not try to explain everything so that you can comprehend all of the details involved and how to use those details practically. Rather, it tries to show you what is in the text in a way that you could easily understand. Then, with someone who does know the grammar, you can easily use these great living trees of grammar as a basis for learning the language. And again, you can get a very extensive explanation in writing that will clarify all of the points that are skipped over in this guide by reading my standard references to Tibetan grammar.

——— ◆◆◆ ———

The most important thing to understand here is that Yangchen Drubpay Dorje's *Great Living Tree* texts are commentaries to Thumi Sambhota's primary definition of Tibetan grammar called *The Root of Grammar, Thirty Verses*. Thumi's primary definition of Tibetan grammar is not taken up with the things that English speakers would expect from their knowledge of English grammar. Rather, it is taken up with explanations of the most important part of Tibetan language, a part of speech called "phrase linkers". Thumi clearly states in his fundamental work that knowing phrase linkers is the master key to knowing to the language. Therefore, Yangchen Drubpay Dorje writes his text in the same way.

You might wonder, "Well, exactly what is contained in Thumi's first treatise?" It has this arrangement:

1. prefatory material;
2. definition of the lettering set;
3. definition of how those letters are used to make words

4. definition of how those letters are used to make the phrase linkers that allow the words of the language to be joined up into meaningful expressions;
5. concluding advice.

The bulk of Thumi's first grammar text is taken up with the fourth section, the section on what are called ཚིག་ཕྲད་ "phrase linkers" or ཕྲད་ "linkers" for short. Therefore, this and other texts following his first text are concerned almost entirely with presentations of one linker after another.

This will doubtless seem uninteresting to a Western eye and will possibly not even seem like a complete explanation of grammar. It is true that this explanation of the phrase linkers is not a complete explanation of grammar; after all, Thumi wrote eight treatises to define Tibetan grammar and the one we are talking about here is only the first. However, this explanation is the explanation that lies at the root of grammar. Understanding phrase linkers is fundamental to understanding the language. Therefore, while this presentation of one linker after another might not be a complete explanation of grammar, it is the explanation of the most fundamental subject of grammar. Therefore, whether you find it interesting or not, this is the way to learn the grammar, at least according to the person who invented it.

What then are these ཚིག་ཕྲད་ phrase linkers? Westerners have called them "particles" for a long time. However, that is a major error. Firstly, the name "particle" is a very old grammatical name for certain parts of English speech. These parts of speech do not correspond at all to the Tibetan parts of speech called "phrase linkers". Secondly, phrase linkers do have their own name in Tibetan and that name was given according to their function. They are specific parts of speech that join up with other words to link groups of words together. They link phrases together and that is their name.

Thumi says very clearly in his concluding advice that knowing what the linkers are and how to use them is the key to the whole language. That is why most of his text his taken up with them and why most of Yangchen Drubpay Dorje's text is taken up with them. In fact, most Tibetan grammar texts spend most of their time on the phrase linkers for the very fact that learning what they are and how to use them is the very root of the Tibetan language.

You might find this hard to believe if you have read Western books about Tibetan grammar but the sad truth is that most books by Westerners about Tibetan grammar do not present Tibetan grammar but a Western idea of it. If you learn Tibetan grammar according to how the inventor of that grammar system says you should, you will find that you will understand the system easily and very clearly. Therefore, the way to learn grammar is to follow what Thumi presented in his fundamental grammar text, *The Thirty Verses*. If you look back at the outline above, you will see that that means that first you have to learn the letters, then you have to understand how those letters make words, and then you have to spend a lot of time on the phrase linkers.

———— ◆◆◆ ————

The Great Living Tree has this for its prefatory material:

- Namo Guru Mañjughoṣhaya.

  I respectfully bow to the supreme guru
  Who is inseparable from Mañjughoṣha and

Having done so, will explain in a brief way
The essence of Thonmi's fine explanation, *The Thirty*.

The first line is a homage in Sanskrit. With it, he pays respect to the source of his knowledge of grammar, his guru Ngulchu Dharmabhadra. He sees him as inseparable with Mañjughoṣha, the particular form of Mañjuśhrī who is the enlightened speech aspect of all the buddhas. In other words, he sees him as the perfect source of all knowledge connected with speech, which is what is needed here.

The first two lines of the verse following that say the same thing.

The last two lines of the verse are a declaration of his intention. This is the same as the tradition in English of stating your intention in writing a book right at the very beginning of the book. He is telling us that the reason for his writing this text is to state the essential points of Thum Sambhota's fundamental grammar text *The Thirty Verses*.

That is the end of the prefatory material. Most of what follows the prefatory material is the body of the text and there is a small conclusion at the end in the form of a verse of poetry.

——— ◆◆◆ ———

The first section of the body of the text is the explanation of the letters of the language:

- The exhibitors of vowel function
  Are the four ཨི་, ཨུ་, ཨེ་, and ཨོ་.
  The consonants are the thirty of ཀ་ and so on.

Thumi Sambhota spent years in India learning Indian languages so that he could formalize the existing, spoken Tibetan language. The formalized language that he invented was not a copy of the Indian Sanskrit language but it was influenced by Sanskrit in many ways. In Sanskrit, letters are defined as the basic sounds of the language. In Sanskrit, it is also defined that there are two types of letters and only two types. The two types of letter are called vowels and consonants. His definition of the letters of Tibetan language is similar to the definition of letters in the Sanskrit language.

In *The Thirty*, Thumi does not define how many vowels there are or how many consonants. Rather, he defines how many written marks there are for the vowels and how many for the consonants. Thumi defines that there are four marks used in writing to show up, that is, to exhibit, the actual functioning of vowels, that is, their sounds. And he defines that there are thirty marks to be used in the Tibetan system of writing to show up the sounds of the consonants.

Yangchen Drubpay Dorje's definition of the vowels and consonants is almost an exact copy of Thumi Sambhota's definition. There has been a great deal of argument over this definition amongst Tibetan grammarians because it is very terse and leaves many things unsaid. However, practically speaking, there are five spoken vowel sounds in Tibetan, with only four of them having a written mark to show their presence. The remaining vowel is known through the absence of any of these marks. It is important to note how that has just been said. Some bad translations of the explanation of this section in *The Fine Explanation Great Living Tree* state that "one vowel is hidden" but that is not at all what the Tibetan says. It says that four vowels are known by way of a mark that shows their presence and one is known by the absence of a mark. This might seem of little account but it is a crucial point when deeper discussions are entered. No-one anywhere in Tibetan history has ever said that "there is a hidden vowel" in the language and especially, no-one has every claimed that there is a hidden vowel in the consonants. This way of talking comes about solely because of Westerners mis-reading these texts then inventing an explanation of Tibetan grammar that simply does not exist in Tibetan grammar!

The five vowels of Tibetan language correspond roughly to the five English vowels a, e, i, o, and u. The first vowel a is the one that does not have a written mark but is known by the absence of a written mark. The other four have these written marks: ི ུ ེ ོ . In order, these marks represent the vowels that correspond roughly to the English vowels i, u, e, and o.

You might wonder why the vowels are written as ཨི་, ཨུ་, ཨེ་, and ཨོ་ by Yangchen Drubpay Dorje and not just as the pure vowel marks shown just above. It is because, in Tibetan, a vowel sound cannot function without a consonant. Therefore, you cannot do what I have just done and write the vowel marks alone. They are unintelligible as such. They have to be written together with a consonant to be meaningful. The Tibetan consonant ཨ is a consonant that has the basic vowel sound "a". Therefore, if you write that first and then put a vowel mark with it, you get a correct representation of the vowel sound. That explains why the vowels are written out the way they are and it also demonstrates that, unlike English, Tibetan vowels always have to be written together with a consonant. The consonant is always written first and the vowel is applied to that because the consonant provides the basic sound and the vowel provides a variation of tone on top of that sound. In other words, in the Tibetan system, a vowel is a modifier of a consonant and cannot function as a letter in its own right.

Then, there are thirty consonants, each one having its own written mark. The consonants are grouped into sets of fours with the last set having only two consonants in it.

The next section moves on to show how the words of Tibetan language are made from the letters of the language. The words of the Tibetan language are not constructed like the words of English.[25]

1. Tibetan words are built around a base letter. The base letter can be any of the thirty consonants.
2. The base letter must have a suffix letter following it. The suffix letter cannot be chosen from the thirty consonants, it has to be chosen from a set of ten consonants defined by Thumi.
3. Then, under certain circumstances a letter can be prefixed to the base letter. The prefix letter cannot be any of the thirty consonants; it must be one of a set of five consonants defined by Thumi.
4. Then, under certain circumstances, a suffix letter can be positioned after an existing suffix. This is called "re-suffixing". There are two specific suffix letters

[25] The entire system of word production with all of the points mentioned immediately below is explained in the first volume of the standard references to Tibetan grammar mentioned in the introduction.

> from among the ten suffix letters which can be used for this purpose.

It is also possible to add letters above and below the base letter, as superfixes and sub-fixes, when making words. These super- and sub-fix letters are not defined in Thumi's treatises. Nonetheless, we know the rules through oral tradition and through the writings of very early grammarians of the eleventh century. These super- and sub-fix letters are regarded as being part of the base letter of the word. When there are super- or sub-fix letters, the main base letter is called the principal base letter and the affixes to it are called the complement base letters.

Thus, Tibetan words are created using a "three slot system". There is always a base letter, that always has a suffix letter, and it might have a prefix letter. If there is a re-suffix letter, it is considered to be an extension of the suffix letter, so does not count as another, fourth, position. This is why the name for these letters in Tibetan is correctly understood to be "re-suffix" and not "post-suffix" as they have mistakenly been called.

The base, suffix, and prefix letters cannot be chosen at random. There is a very complicated set of rules for which suffixes (and re-suffixes) and prefixes can be used with which base letter. These rules follow on from the fact that each letter is also assigned a gender value. The details of letter gender and how it affects word production and other matters are written up in Thumi's sixth treatise *The Application of Gender Signs*.

As mentioned, the gender-based rules for word production in the Tibetan language are very complicated. Very few Tibetans understand them. Fortunately, one does not have to learn these rules or even know about them because the work was done long ago of making up every single word possible in accordance with the rules. There are about six thousand single Tibetan words possible according to the rules of letter gender. These have already been constructed and put into use and no more are possible!

This situation has an interesting effect on how Tibetan language is learned. Because all of the possible single words for the language have been made and put into use already, Tibetans do not learn rules for making words. Instead, they simply learn all the single words of the language. It is very doable because the total number of words is relatively small.

Yangchen Drubpay Dorje summarizes all of the above in the following words:

- ག་ང་ད་ན་བ་མ་འ་ར་ལ་ and ས་ are the ten suffixes.
ད་ and ས་ both are re-suffixes;
ད་ is obtained with ན་ར་ལ་ and
ས་ is obtained with ག་ང་བ་ and མ་.
ག་ད་བ་མ་ and འ་ are the prefixes.

He defines the ten suffixes, then the two re-suffix letters and when they are to be used, and then the five prefixes. This is not arbitrary: Tibetan words are built starting with a base letter, then the suffixes are added, then the prefixes are added. Thumi advises in *The Thirty Verses* that the suffixes are the key to the whole language. The reason for their being the key is taken up in the longer commentaries, for example, in *Situ's Words*. It is because the linkers, which are the pieces that hold the language together, are constructed from the suffixes.

The next section takes up most of the text. It is an explanation of the main types of linkers.

There are two types of linkers: dependent and independent. The *Thirty Verses* deals first with several dependent linkers and then with several independent linkers. Therefore, Yangchen Drubpay Dorje does the same.

Dependent linkers have a spelling which is dependent on the word which they follow. Specifically, the suffix letter that ends a word controls the spelling of the phrase linker that will follow it. That is why they are called "dependent" linkers.

There are ten suffixes and there is also the situation of a hidden suffix. What does that mean? According to *The Thirty Verses*, every word has to have one of the ten suffixes. However, two hundred years after Thumi Sambhota, a rule was made that in some circumstances suffixes and re-suffixes do not have to be written explicitly, though they do have to be understood to be present. Thus, there are ten ending letters corresponding to the ten suffixes being present and written out and there is one what is called "no-ending letter" when one of the ten suffixes is there but not written out.

Because dependent linkers have to match the ending of the word to which they are going to be linked, each type of linker has to consist of a group of linkers, each with a different spelling. Therefore, each type of dependent linker has to be defined in three ways. Firstly, the functions of that type of linker have to be defined; some linkers have only one function and some linkers have several functions. Secondly, each type of dependent linker will have to be a group of linkers, each with a different spelling, and each of the linkers in that group will have to be presented. Thirdly, there has to be a definition of which member of the linker set will be used after which word ending. If you look at the dependent linker definitions, you will find that these three aspects are always presented. To become good with Tibetan language, you do have to commit all of this to memory. If you do not, you will not be good at the language. It is that simple.

——— ◆◆◆ ———

The first dependent linker is the equivalent of a full stop in English though it can also function as the verb to be plus full stop.[26]

- གོ་ངོ་དོ་ནོ་བོ་མོ་འོ་རོ་ལོ་སོ་ and ཏོ་ are the concluders,
  Also called completing words and coupled concluders.
  ཏོ is connected when there is a forceful ending; འོ when
  there is no ending;
  And the others to be concordant with the suffix at
  name's ending.

This type of linker has three names in Tibetan grammar: "concluder" was the name given by Thumi Sambhota; and "completing words" and "coupled concluders" were names coined by later grammarians. You will see that there are eleven members in the set corresponding to the eleven types of possible word ending. You will see that the rules for the use of the eleven are provided. Note that a forceful ending is a grammatical term; it

[26] In U.S. English, a full stop is called a "period".

means an re-suffix ending letter. It is so-named because its presence causes the word to which it is re-suffixed to be pronounced with more force.

——— ◆◆◆ ———

The next set of linkers are called the "la equivalents" because the one letter "la" can, roughly speaking, be used in place of all them. Thus, they are *equivalent* to the phrase linker *la*.

- སུ་རུ་ར་དུ་ན་ལ་ and ཏུ་ are the seven la-equivalents;
  They are used for cases two, four, and seven,
  And with identity and timing.
  ས་ gets སུ་; ག་བ་ and forceful ད་ get ཏུ་;
  ང་ད་ན་མ་ར་ and ལ་ get དུ་;
  And འ་ and no ending get ར་ and རུ་.

Note that this type of linker has multiple functions. They are all case functions. Tibetan language has cases of nouns exactly the same way as English has cases of nouns. There are eight cases in Tibetan grammar and these correspond roughly to the English cases. It is not mentioned here but there are also some non-case functions for some of the members of this set. Note again how there is a definition of the members comprising the set, what the functions are of the set, and how the individual members are to be applied to the various eleven possible word endings.

Note that ར་ and རུ་ can also be markers of adverbial function. Also, ལ་ can be a marker of the end of a clause. These are not mentioned here but it is important to know, otherwise a major error can occur.

——— ◆◆◆ ———

Next, the following dependent linkers are presented: connective and agentive cases; ornament and inclusion; continuatives; and separation and inclusion. These have already been clearly explained in the root *Great Living Tree* and are also explained in the glossary.

Note that the continuative linkers do not have simple parts-of-speech equivalents in the English language. More than with any other Tibetan part of speech, you need to gain first-hand experience with them under the tutelage of a teacher who both understands continuatives from the Tibetan perspective and understands all the different ways that they can come out in English. Briefly, the continuatives can correspond not only to words in English but various phrasings such as "—that is, xxx—" and others; to punctuation marks such as commas, semi-colons, em- and n-dashes; and to verb tense modifiers, for example changing "did" to "having done"; and so on. Because of the lack of direct correspondence with a specific part of speech in English, these are among the hardest parts of Tibetan speech to know how to translate.

- ར་ and རུ་; འི་ and ཡི་; འང་ and ཡང་ are distinguished
Respectively as not verse padding and padding.
འོ་ and འུ་ and འམ་ with and without
A prior tsheg are also like that.

When a line of verse does not need padding, the འོ་ of concluders, the འུ་ of names, and the འམ་ of separation-inclusion do not get a tsheg before them as in དཔལ་ལྡན་ལྷ་མོའོ།. At this point, Yangchen Drubpay Dorje reviews a special usage that exists with the la-equivalent members ར་ and རུ་, with the connective case members འི་ and ཡི་, and with the ornamenting and inclusion members འང་ and ཡང་ that have just been defined. In each of these three cases, it is possible either to join the first member mentioned onto the preceding word or to write a break mark after the word and then to write the second member mentioned. Thus, one could write པར་ or པ་རུ་, and པའི་ or པ་ཡི་, and པའང་ or པ་ཡང་. The meaning would be the same in each case. The reason for having this possibility is that it gives an author the means to construct verse lines of the desired length. Therefore, this principle in general is called "verse padding" and "non-padding". This is mentioned in *The Thirty*.

It is not mentioned in *The Thirty* but Yangchen Drubpay Dorje does a good job of making it clear that the same sort of thing applies with the concluding linker འོ་ and separation and inclusion linker འམ་ which have also just been defined, as well as with the linker འུ་ which has not been defined so far. For example, one can write པ་འོ་ or པའོ་, and ཀའུ་ or ཀ་འུ་, and པའམ་ or པ་འམ་. There is no change in meaning but there is a change in the number of words on a line in each case. Therefore, this provides a technique for constructing lines of verse of exactly the right length. The linker འུ་, when positioned after another word, changes the meaning of that word to "a small version of" the thing mentioned by the word.

———— ◆◆◆ ————

- ནས་ and ལས་ source, segregate, and include.
  For actual source, either one may be connected;

Concordant-class segregation gets ནས་ and non-
concordant ལས་;
For inclusion only the term ནས་ is used.

Following that, the source linkers ནས་ and ལས་ are defined. They have both what is called "true" or "actual" source functions and sub-sets of that function called segregation and inclusion. Some of the preceding linkers have had multiple, differing functions defined. Here there is one function, the function of source, being defined. There is the main function of actual source and two variants of that function. It is important to note that these are variations of the one function and not differing functions.

That completes the section on dependent linkers.

——— ◆◆◆ ———

Now several independent linkers are defined. Because independent linkers are not controlled by the letter at the end of the word to which the linker will be attached, they are independent linkers. This simplifies their definition because only their function has to be defined.

——— ◆◆◆ ———

The first independent linker is the calling or hailing linker.

- ཀྱེ་ and ཀ་ཡེ་ are calling terms.
  They are mostly connected ahead of the names.

In fact, there are several more calling linkers. They are needed because there are levels of honorific to be observed. It is the same as in English where, for example, you would not say, "Hey You!"

to the president of a country. Instead, you would use the appropriately honorific language for hailing him, such as "O Mr. President". Likewise, in Tibetan, there are several terms for calling, each with its own level of honorific.

The calling linkers are mostly positioned ahead of the rest of what is to be said, the same as happenings with hailing someone in English. However, on occasion they can be put at the end of what is to be said, again, as can be done in English. For example, in English we can say, "You! Go over there", but we can also say, "Go over there, you!"

◆◆◆

- ནི་ is a term of segregation and of highlighting.
  དང་ has the five uses of inclusion, separation, reason,
  Timing, and instruction.

Then the linkers ནི་ and དང་ are mentioned. Note the multiple definitions for both. Their Tibetan definitions must be properly known if they are to be translated correctly. For example ནི་ has often been thought merely to provide padding and have no meaning further than that. However, while it is true that it can function as padding, especially in verse, it has the two other functions mentioned above which are, in general, its more common usages. And, while non-Tibetans usually learn quickly that དང་ means "and" in English, they often do not understand its other four main functions, which can lead to major errors in translation.

◆◆◆

- The དེ་ term at the beginning of a name
  Has the two uses of immediately preceding convention
  And accounting for something else.

Then the དེ་ linker is mentioned. This is spelled and pronounced the same as the དེ་ already defined as a continuative linker. However, this is a case of what would be called in English grammar "one word with two entirely different meanings". It is not mentioned here, but this linker has a complementary linker that goes with it: འདི་. The former is roughly equivalent to "that" and the latter to "this", though this pair of terms can be equivalent to other English pronouns as well, such as "it".

——— ◆◆◆ ———

Then Yangchen Drubpay Dorje does well by mentioning several linkers that are combined with other terms to give many different linkers, most of which are not mentioned in *The Thirty*. He says,

- ཅི་ཇི་སུ་ and གང་ are terms of generality:
  ཅི་ with ཞིག་སྟེ་སླད་འདྲ་ and ཕྱིར་;
  ཇི་ with སྙེད་སྲིད་ལྟར་བཞིན་ and སྐད་;
  སུ་ to persons; and གང་ to all.

Note that all four terms in the first line can be both interrogative and non-interrogative. Accordingly, their various compounds shown in the following lines can be interrogative as well as non-interrogative. In the fourth line, the first term is only ever who or whom or who? or whom? because it is only ever used for living beings and the second term is equivalent to which or what or which? or what? and also to who and whom and who? and whom? Because it can be used when referencing both living and non-living things.

It would take too long to explain all of the possible combinations of the terms he has mentioned, so that will not be done here.

——— ◆◆◆ ———

Then he defines the terms of the owner. A term of the owner is created by adding one of three Tibetan letters to the end of a word. The combination of the word plus letter now has the sense of a person or thing connected with the meaning of the word to which the letter was added. There are some rules about when to use these letters. The rules are complicated by the fact that some words already have one of these letters in place in which case a further letter has to be added.

- པ་བ་ and མ་ with and without naro are terms of the owner.
  At ག་ད་ན་བ་མ་ས་ and forceful endings, པ་ is obtained.
  At ང་འ་ར་ and ལ་ for terms of the owner that become far, བ་,
  And for parts, the connection of པ་ is good.
  པ་ and བ་ at name endings also are mostly like that.
  མ་ is indefinite, connect it as required.

It does not mention it here but there are gender considerations with the use of the three terms. Generally speaking, the addition of པ་ makes the combination male, the addition of བ་ makes it neutral meaning that it can be either or both male and female, and the addition of མ་ makes it female.

——— ◆◆◆ ———

Then he defines the terms used to negate.

- མ་མི་མིན་ and མེད་ are terms of negation.

> མ་ and མི་ ahead, མིན་ and མེད་ at the end,
> And མ་ as an in-between-consonant as well.

The first two are used before the words that they will negate and the latter two are used after. In addition, མ་ can be used in between two words as a way of negating both, as shown in the examples in *Fine Explanation Great Living Tree*.

——— ◆◆◆ ———

Then he defines several dependent linkers which are not mentioned in *Thirty Verses* but which are very common in the language and some of which have exceptions that need to be learned.

- As for the phrase linkers ཞིང་ and so on:
  ང་ན་མ་འ་ར་ལ་ endings and no ending get ཞིང་ཞེས་ཞེ་འོ་ཞེ་ན་ ཞིག་;
  ག་ད་བ་ and forceful ད་ endings get ཅིང་ཅེས་ཅེ་འོ་ཅེ་ན་ཅིག་;
  ས་ endings, except for special ཞེས་, get ཤིང་ཤིག་ཤེ་འོ་ཤེ་ན་.
  However, in ཁ་ཅིག་, ལྷན་ཅིག་, and so on,
  They are part of a name so take care not to err!

In the last two lines, he points out that the particular term ཅིག་ is not necessarily a linker but can also be part of a standard word so cautions not to make a mistake about it. In fact, some of the other linkers mentioned are not only linkers but also are words. All of these have to be learned so that a mistake is not made.

——— ◆◆◆ ———

Now we have reached the conclusion. When he says,

- When a bare letter is fronted, an ending འ་ is required;

With a hook, bend, superfix, or subfix it is dropped ...

he is actually re-phrasing information given in the first section of the conclusion of the *Thirty Verses*. In that section, Thumi gives the rule that any word, meaning any word other than a linker, has to have a suffix. If there is no suffix as part of the word, then a suffix ending of འ་ has to be added. Now if a prefix is also added to the word, that ending འ་ has to stay in place but if the base letter of the word has a hook, bend, superfix, or subfix then the ending འ་ does not have to be written. This is true but it is a complicated way to understand the situation. There is no easy way to lay out the whole thing but there are better ways, I think, to explain it. This is dealt with at length in my first standard reference on grammar.

——— ◆◆◆ ———

- In prose where there is much meaning, at the boundary of a name;
  To divide medium meanings; at completed lesser meanings;
  And in verse at an ending ག།, a single shad should be made.
  Prose ending in a completing word and
  Verse at the end of a line gets two shad.
  At the completion of a great section of meaning and
  At the close of a chapter, four shad are required.
  Except for letter ང་, there is no tsheg between a letter and a shad.

Next he provides some information on how to apply the two main punctuation marks of Tibetan language: the tsheg mark which is normally written between two words similar to how a space is left between words in English and the shad stroke which is used as a major break like the comma, full stop, and so on of English. Again, Thumi does not mention this in his *Thirty Verses* but it is something that a beginner does need to become familiar with, so Yangchen Drubpay Dorje is doing a good job again by presenting this information.

The rules for the use of tsheg's and shad's are clearly stated though just reading about them is not enough. One needs to gain practice at reading and writing the language in order to get a proper feel for the use of these punctuation marks.

——— ◆◆◆ ———

Then he says,

- Make conscientious efforts at gaining a precise understanding of those and the rest of the topics of grammar!

This is his advice to learn the basics of the language that have just been presented until you are thoroughly competent with them and then to read texts that have more detailed explanations of grammar in order to further your understanding. Thumi adds in his conclusion that you should do what you have to do to get the level of proficiency that you need for whatever studies you want to undertake and that you should not stop learning the language and its grammar until you have reached that point.

I would add my own encouragement to that. These beginners texts open the door to Tibetan grammar but they are not do-it-yourself texts that contain everything needed. Rather, they are meant to be a basis for learning gained through relating to someone who does have full knowledge of the subject and who is willing to pass it on to you. I have done this myself by being willing to spend long periods in North India under very difficult conditions in order to hear complete teachings on grammar—all spoken in Tibetan and without any English as a prop—from my teacher Pema Gyaltsen who was, till his death, acknowledged as the greatest of present-day Tibetan grammarians. It took years of hard work to learn Tibetan well enough just to be able to get that kind of instruction and it took a lot of personal sacrifice to go there and live in the extremely difficult conditions that I was confronted with. However, by being willing to do all that and then being totally respectful to my teacher, I obtained a knowledge of Tibetan grammar beyond what most learned Tibetans have. One result of that is that I can write about it for the sake of others, something which is very pleasing to do. Another result is that translation work is almost effortless for me; I can pick up a text, read it, and dictate the translation on the spot. However, the best result of mastering Tibetan grammar by far is that the door to Tibetan literature in the fields that I want to study—the profound Buddhadharma—has been opened completely.

What I have said there in my own words and based on my own experience is exactly what Thumi Sambhota talks about in his conclusion to his *Thirty Verses*. He says that you learn the letters, then you learn to read the words, then you learn the phrase linkers, and then you learn to understand the written word as a whole. That ability, once gained, is only a tool, he says, but a very important tool. It is the tool that you need in order to be able to learn and then gain mastery in whatever field of knowledge interests you. He says to learn Tibetan language following exactly that procedure and then, once you have learned it, to find a teacher, learn the words of your area of interest from him, contemplate their meaning, and finally gain the fruit of realization. How true it is! I can only encourage you to persevere with your Tibetan studies and then use them to learn and master your field of interest, especially the field of practising Buddha's dharma for the sake of releasing every single being from the profound misery of cyclic existence.

Yangchen Drubpay Dorje ends by expressing his theme of a grand tree in the forest of trees that explain Tibetan language, a tree that stands above all others with the excellence of its explanation. He says,

- This great living tree of fine explanation
  Which is not obscured by a leafiness of words
  And has fruits of meaning ripe to eat
  Was propagated by Yangchen Drubpay Dorje.

GLOSSARY OF TERMS

This is a glossary of grammar terms used in this book. A short but clear definition of each term is given. Extensive definitions of all the Tibetan parts of speech are given in the two volumes of the standard references to Tibetan grammar mentioned in the introduction and those treatises are strongly recommended for those wanting a complete explanation of the Tibetan grammar terms.

Accounting for something else, Tib. rnam grangs gzhan can: This phrase indicates the function of what is called a pronoun in English.

Actual source, Tib. 'byung khung dngos: This is the name for the actual source case, given to distinguish it from the one subdivision that exists for the source case. See under "source case".

Agentive term, Tib. byed sgra: This is an abbreviation of "term of the agent" *q.v.*

Ali, Skt. āli: The name in Sanskrit for the vowel set. It literally means "the *string* of vowels starting with *ā*".

Bare letter, Tib. yig ge rkyang pa: A bare letter is any consonant letter of the alphabet to which another letter—either super- or sub-fix—has not been affixed. E.g., ག་ is the bare letter "ga" whereas the letter "ga" with superfixed sa and subfixed ra སྒྲ་ is not a bare letter.

Beginning of a name, Tib. ming gi thog ma: This refers to the position immediately before any given grammatical name.

Bend: Tib. kyed: This is a poetic term for the ེ "drengbu" vowel sign.

Boundary of a name, Tib. ming mtshams: This refers to the position immediately after any given grammatical name.

Calling terms, Tib. bod sgra: This is an abbreviation of "term of calling" *q.v.*

Case, Tib. rnam dbye: Tibetan language has grammar cases which are very similar to English grammar cases but not the same as Tibetan cases, therefore an comprehensive effort to match the names of Tibetan cases with English ones has not been made.

Cases in Tibetan grammar, as in English grammar, show the relationship between a noun and other parts of a sentence. There are eight cases in Tibetan grammar, though sometimes the first, which is the noun itself without any further case sign added, is left out to give seven. The cases are: 1) the noun itself with no further relationship to anything else shown; 2) the objective case, also called "site of a function", meaning that shows the place where intransitive action occurs is shown; 3) the agentive case, meaning that the agent of a transitive action is shown; 4) the purposive case, also called "necessity and purpose", meaning that a relationship to some object is shown in which some need or purpose on the side of the object is shown; 5) the source case meaning that the source of something is shown; 6) the connective case, meaning that a relationship between two things is shown; 7) the locative case, also called "site of support", meaning that the place which is a basis for something is shown; and 8) the calling case, which indicates that another being is being called or hailed.

There are two sub-division cases: 1) the second case has a sub-division called "identity" and 2) the seventh case has a sub-division called "timing". According to *Situ's Words*, the first means "at the time of something being acted on and something acting, the object and action are one entity, as in 'od du 'tsher ba (radiating light)" and the second means "when they are connected to have the meaning expressing time, as in nyi ma shar ba na chos ston (teaching the dharma when the sun rises)".

Completing word, Tib. rdzogs tshig: This is one of three names for the set of phrase linkers which are used to show that a sentence has been completed. The other terms are "concluder" and "coupled concluder".

Concluder, Tib. slar bsdu: See under "completing word".

Concordant bases, Tib. mthun pa'i gzhi: This phrase is used to indicate that two items are of the same type or belong to the same category of thing.

Concordant-class segregation, Tib. mthun pa'i dgar ba: This is the name of one aspect of the subdivision of the fifth or source case *q.v.* It has a matching aspect called non-concordant-class segregation.

Connection, Tib. sbyor ba: The general name for the process in which the parts of speech are built up from letters. Letters are connected to produces the basic parts of speech—grammatical names and grammatical phrases—of the Tibetan language.

Connective term, Tib. 'brel sgra: This is an abbreviation of "term of connection" *q.v.*

Consonant, Tib. gsal byed: The Tibetan lettering set is composed of two types of letters, no more and no less: vowels and consonants. The name for a consonant in Tibetan, gsal byed, means that the consonant "clearly produces" a sound of its own so that it can be readily distinguished from all other consonants.

Continuative, Tib. lhag bcas: This is the name of a set of three phrase linkers which, by definition, function to show that there is more to come.

Convention, Tib. tha snyad: This term is defined as meaning any verbal or mental construct which has been agreed upon as the signifier of a particular meaning. For example, "red"—both the concept and the word, whether written or spoken—is the convention used to indicate the colour red.

Coupled concluder, Tib. zla sdud: See under "completing word". This term gets its name from the fact that, as the type of term which concludes a sentence, it has its spelling matched to, so is coupled with, the preceding word.

Dependent linker, Tib. gzhan dbang gi prad: This is the name for one of the two types of phrase linker, the other being the independent linker. See under "linker" for more.

Differentiating tsheg, Tib. phyed tsheg: A letter ང་ nga followed by a । shad stroke must have a ་ tsheg punctuation mark placed in between the letter nga and the shad. The tsheg ensures that the ང། nga shad combination is not mistaken for a letter

བ ba, which it easily can be without the added tsheg. Thus, this tsheg is called a differentiating tsheg because it differentiates the nga shad combination from a ba letter.

The *Fine Explanation Great Living Tree* explains: "It is required between a final letter nga and a shad in order to prevent the possibility of that construction being mistaken for a ba letter, for example in མ་བསྒྲིབས་ཤིང་།. Other letter-shad combinations do not have a tsheg inserted in between them, for example in གཡུར་ཟ་བའི།".

Drengbu, Tib. greng bu: This is the name, literally meaning "a small swash", of the second of the four Tibetan vowels, having a sound similar to "e".

Ending, Tib. mtha': This is the general name for any letter added in either the suffix or re-suffix position to a name-base letter. In other words, it is the final or ending letter of the intertsheg under consideration.

An intertsheg by definition always has an ending letter. However, new rules that were introduced in the language revisions allowed for certain endings not to be written. Therefore, "no ending" is discussed for those cases where no apparent ending is present, even if, grammatically speaking, there is an ending letter.

A "name's ending" is the ending letter on a grammatical name.

Five prefixes, Tib. sngon 'jug lnga: The prefix letters are a set of five letters. They are derived from the set of ten suffix letters.

Five uses of inclusion, separation, reason, timing, and verbal instruction, Tib. sdud, 'byed, rgyu mtshan, tshe skabs, gdams ngag: These are the names of the five different functions defined for the དང་ dang term.

Four exhibitors of the function of the ali vowels, Tib. dbyangs bzhi'i bya ba gsal bar byed pa: There are four written signs used to indicate the function of the Tibetan vowels. Although there is a fifth vowel sound in the Tibetan language, no sign is needed to indicate it. It is the vowel "a". See also "Āli".

Forceful ending, Tib. drag mtha': The letters ད་ and ས་ can be used in the re-suffix position. In that cases, they are in the ending position of the intertsheg of which they are a part and cause the pronunciation of the intertsheg to be markedly strengthened. Therefore, they are called "forceful endings".

Forceful ད་ endings, Tib. da drag: See under forceful ending.

Forceful ས་ endings, Tib. sa drag: See under forceful ending.

Fronted, Tib. 'phul ba: This term used to indicate that an intertsheg has a prefix on it. See also "fronting".

Fronting, Tib. 'phul rten: This is the general name for all prefix letters given that they push into an intertsheg from the front.

Four vowels, Tib. dbyangs bzhi: Thumi Saṃbhoṭa states only that there are four written marks used to indicate the function of vowels. None of his remaining treatises on grammar (only two of the original eight are extant) discusses how many vowel sounds there are in the language. This has led to a great deal of debate amongst Tibetan grammarians over the centuries. In recent times, some Westerners have claimed that there is a fifth "hidden" vowel but that exceeds that the system itself says. In fact, there are five vowels sounds. However, it is a mistake to say that the fifth one is "hidden". It is not hidden but is a part of the pronunciation of consonants that does not need a written mark to indicate its presence.

Gender Signs, Tib. rtags: Tibetan grammar assigns gender to the letters of the alphabet. The genders affect pronunciation and several other aspects of the language. The system of letter gender and its application are defined in Thumi Saṃbhoṭa's treatise called *Application of Gender Signs*.

Gigu, Tib. gi gu: This is the name, literally meaning "bent over gi", of the first of the four Tibetan vowels. It has a bent over shape and having a sound similar to "i", hence its name.

Grammatical name, Tib. ming: This is a longer term for what is simply called a "name" in Tibetan grammar. The word "grammatical" has been added to make it clear that this is not a name in the usual English sense but a name in the specific Tibetan grammatical sense.

Grammatical phrase, Tib. tshig: This is a longer term for what is simply called a "phrase" in Tibetan grammar. The word "grammatical" has been added to make it clear that this is not a phrase in the usual English sense but a phrase in the specific Tibetan grammatical sense.

Hook, Tib. gug: This is a poetic name for the gigu vowel letter.

Identity, Tib. ngo bo: This is the name of the one sub-division of the second case. See under "case".

Immediately preceding convention, Tib. tha snyad 'das ma thags pa: A phrase used when discussing the function of the དེ་ term. It is one of several pronoun-type functions performed by this term. "Convention" refers to a spoken or written term of language which beings have agreed on to have a certain meaning.

Inclusion, Tib. sdud: There are three types of inclusion function defined in Tibetan grammar. They are carried out by a non-case linker called a separation-inclusion linker, a set of non-case linkers called ornament-inclusion linkers, and a case linker of the fifth case called a segregation-inclusion linker.

Independent linker, Tib. rang dbang gi prad: This is one of two types of phrase linker, the other being the dependent linker. See under "linker" for more.

Intertsheg, Tib. tsheg bar: The base morpheme of the English language is the word. Tibetan language has not one but two base morphemes—grammatical names and phrase linkers. The two have very different functions, but they share one morphological feature, which is that they are written with a tsheg punctuation mark on either side of them. Thus, the name for a basic unit of speech in Tibetan language is not a "word" but an "intertsheg".

Note that these have mistakenly been called "syllables" in English. This happened because they were thought to be similar to syllables of the English language. That is mistaken.

Internal divisions of cases, Tib. rnam dbye'i nang gses: Two internal divisions or sub-divisions of Tibetan cases are formally defined. See under "case" for more.

Intransitive verb, Tib. tha mi dad pa'i bya tshig: Tibetan verbs are defined as being either transitive or intransitive. The definition of transitive and intransitive is very similar to that of English grammar.

Kali, Skt. kāli: The name in Sanskrit for the consonant set. It literally means "the *string* of consonants starting with *ka*".

La equivalent, Tib. la don: "La equivalent" is the name given to one set of phrase linkers which collectively perform several linking functions. Unlike with some other linkers, the name "la equivalent" does not refer to any of the functions performed but indicates that the single letter ལ་ la can perform all of the functions of the set of linkers. Thus, the other terms in the set are functionally equivalent to that letter and are given their name on that basis. There are seven la equivalent terms.

Linker, Tib. phrad: "Linker" is the actual meaning of the Tibetan name for what Westerners have mistakenly called a "particle" till now. "Linker" is an abbreviated name; the full name is "phrase linker" «tshig phrad» *q.v.*

Linkers are of two types: dependent linkers and independent linkers. Dependent linkers change their spelling depending on the last letter of the word immediately preceding them. Because of this, each dependent linker actually consists of a group of linkers, each with a different spelling that will match one of the possible letter endings to a preceding word. Independent linkers have a constant spelling which does not change in relation to the last letter of the preceding word. Because of this, each independent linker is a single item, not a group of items with various spellings.

Name, Tib. ming: Tibetan language is built from letters. Letters are connected to each other to form one of two basic parts of speech—grammatical names and phrase linkers. A single phrase linker is then connected to a grammatical name to produce what is called a grammatical phrase. Further names and phrases are connected to form the most complex parts of speech called "expressions".

Name-base, Tib. ming gzhi: Tibetan grammatical names are built from letters. An initial consonant is set in place and it then has any of suffixes, prefixes, super-fixes, sub-fixes, and vowels added to it to make a grammatical name. The initial letter, which is the basis for the name, is thus called "the name-base".

Name's ending, Tib. ming mtha': The ending letter on a grammatical name, which will be either a suffix or re-suffix, is the name's ending. Note that, according to Thumi Saṃbhoṭa's original definition of the language, every grammatical name must have a suffix or re-suffix letter. However, in the revised form of the language that was set in place some two hundred years after that, certain cases of suffixes no longer needed to be written out. This can lead to the mis-perception that some grammatical names—for example ཉ་ nya, the word for fish—do not have a name's ending letter when in fact they do.

Naro, Tib. sna ru and na ro. This is the name of the fourth Tibetan vowel, having a sound similar to "o".

Non-case function, Tib. rnam dbye ma yin pa'i bya ba: A term used to indicate a linker that performs a function which is not a case-marking function.

Non-concordant-class segregation, Tib. mi mthun pa'i dgar ba: This is the name of one aspect of the only subdivision of the fifth or source case *q.v.* It has a matching aspect called concordant-class segregation.

Nga tsheg, Tib. nga tsheg: This is another term for the differentiating tsheg *q.v.*

Ornament and include, Tib. rgyan sdud: The type of phrase linker called an "ornament" has the two functions of ornamenting and including. See also "inclusion" for the thee types of inclusion performed by phrase linkers.

Padding, Tib. kha skong gi yi ge: See under "verse padding".

Particle: This is the name usually given by Westerners to the Tibetan part of speech called a "prad" in Tibetan. The actual meaning of the name is not "particle" but "linker". The word "particle" was in use in English grammar several centuries ago, when it was used to indicate bits of speech that did not have clearly defined functions. In Tibetan grammar, the parts of speech called "linkers" are not poorly defined bits and pieces of the Tibetan language; rather, they were regarded by Thumi Saṃbhoṭa as the most important parts of the language. Therefore, to call them "particles" is not only wrong from the point of view of the meaning of their name, but also because they are not merely bits and pieces but crucial parts of the language. See under "linker" for more.

Phrases, Tib. tshig: Tibetan language is built from letters. Letters are used to build two types of base morpheme, called grammatical names and phrase linkers. When a single phrase linker is applied to a single grammatical name, the resulting structure consisting of two intertshegs is called a "tshig". This term is often translated into English as "word". However, it is not at all like an English word. An English word is a base morpheme of the language whereas a Tibetan "tshig" is not a morpheme of the language but a more complex structure of the language that has been constructed by joining two morphemes of the language together. Moreover, it is a very specific structure, made exactly of one grammatical name and one phrase linker. It is a unique structure of the Tibetan language with no exact match in English. Therefore, because it is similar to an English phrase in that it can stand on its own but is not a complete expression, I have called it a phrase (and also a grammatical phrase in order to clearly distinguish it).

Phrase linkers, Tib. tshig phrad: Tibetan language is built from letters. Letters are connected to each other to form one of two basic parts of speech—grammatical names and phrase linkers. These parts of speech are then connected as needed to form grammatical phrases and then expressions of speech. Phrase (tshig) linkers (phrad) are, according to Thumi Saṃbhoṭa, the linchpins of Tibetan language—he says in *The*

Thirty that, by understanding them properly, anyone can understand the Tibetan language.

Their name in Tibetan is exactly descriptive of their function: they are connected to grammatical names to produce grammatical phrases (Tib. tshig). These grammatical phrases are then used to make complete expressions (sentences). Thus, these parts of speech have the function of sitting in between grammatical names and other intertshegs in order to construct the language. They are exactly "phrase linkers" as their name says in Tibetan.

Phrase linkers have long been called "particles" in English publications about the Tibetan language. This is a mistake that was introduced hundreds of years ago by the first translators of Tibetan language into English and European languages. It is essential to stop calling them by an English grammar term (particle) which does not apply and to start calling them by their correct name according to Tibetan grammar—"phrase linker".

Phrase ornaments of concordance, Tib. mthun pa'i tshig rgyan: The ornament function of the class of phrase linkers called ornaments or phrase ornaments has two sub-divisions: concordant and non-concordant ornamentation.

Phrase ornaments of non-concordance, Tib. mi mthun pa'i tshig rgyan: The ornament function of the class of phrase linkers called ornaments or phrase ornaments has two sub-divisions: concordant and non-concordant ornamentation.

Prefix, Tib. sngon 'jug: The general name for a set of five letters used in name formation. These are the letters which are affixed to the front of the name-base letter. They are also called "frontings" for this reason.

Prose, Tib. tshig lhug: The name for composition not in verse.

Pure Letters, Tib. dag yig: The general name in the vocabulary of Tibetan grammar for any written work that explains the ways of the Tibetan language. It includes all types of work on grammar, dictionaries, and so on.

Recipient, Tib. 'jug yul: The particular construction of letters or the bare letter to which another letter will be connected when forming an intertsheg.

Re-suffix, Tib. yang 'jug: Two of the ten suffix letters, ད་ da and ས་ sa, can be connected to a grammatical name in the position after the suffix position. This position is then called the re-suffix position. These have incorrectly been called post-suffixes in English. A post-suffix would be any letter that follows a suffix. However, that is not the meaning here. These are the suffix letters used yet again in the suffix position. Note that the Tibetan name indicates this, literally saying "again suffix"; note that it does not use the term "post" or "after".

Re-suffix ད, Tib. yang 'jug da: This is the name for the letter da when used as a re-suffix.

Re-suffix ས, Tib. yang 'jug sa: This is the name for the letter sa when used as a re-suffix.

Separate and include, Tib. 'byed sdud: This is the name of a set of phrase linkers that has the two functions of separation and inclusion. See under inclusion for all types of inclusion performed by phrase linkers.

Segregation and of highlighting, Tib. dgar brnan: The phrase linker ནི་ "ni" performs two different functions called "segregation" and "highlighting".

Shad, Tib. shad: This is the name of a vertical stroke used as a punctuation mark. It has several functions. In English grammatical terms, it can function as a comma, semi-colon, and full stop.

Source, Tib. 'byung khung: This is the name of the fifth Tibetan grammatical case. Source has two sub-divisions: 1) actual source and 2) segregation and inclusion. Segregation is further divided into concordant-class and non-concordant-class segregation. See also under "case".

Source, segregate, and include: This refers to the three aspects of the fifth case: actual source case and the segregation and inclusion which are the two aspects of the sub-division of the source case. See under "source".

Speech Door Weapon, Tib. smra sgo mtshon cha: The name of a grammar text written in the eleventh century C.E. by the Indian paṇḍit Smṛitijñānakīrti who moved to Tibet and became expert in Tibetan grammar. The text is frequently quoted by later grammarians.

Suffix Tib. rjes 'jug: This is the general name for a set of ten consonant letters used in grammatical name formation. These are the letters which are affixed to the rear of the name-base letter. Two of them, the letters da and sa, can be affixed followed a suffix and are therefore called "re-suffixes".

Subfix, Tib. btags: There are four possible sub-fix letters when constructing a grammatical name: ya, ra, la, and wa. They are called yatag, ratag, latag, and watag or wazur respectively. See under "Grammatical name construction".

Superfix: Tib. mgo: There are three possible super-fix letters when constructing a grammatical name: ra, la, and sa. They are called rago, lago, and sago respectively. See under "Grammatical name construction".

Ten suffixes, Tib. rjes 'jug bcu: The suffix letters are a set of ten consonants. See under suffix.

Terms of calling, Tib. bod kyi sgra: The name for the phrase linkers which have the function of hailing another person. It is the terms of the vocative case of English grammar. Terms of calling are divided into three: terms used only for hailing persons of higher social standing, terms used only for hailing persons of equal social standing, and terms used only for hailing persons of lesser social standing.

Terms of connection, Tib. 'brel ba'i sgra: The name for the phrase linkers which have the function of showing the connective case, which is the equivalent of the English genitive case.

Terms of the owner, Tib. bdag po'i sgra: The name for the group of phrase linkers which, when joined to a grammatical name, show that it refers to a person or other being. There are male, female, and generic terms of the owner. The term "owner" is a direct translation of the equivalent term in Sanskrit grammar, "pati".

Terms of generality, Tib. spyi'i sgra: The name for a set of phrase linkers which have the function of representing a general class of things or beings.

Terms of the agent, Tib. byed pa'i sgra: The name for the group of phrase linkers which represent the third case. The name is also abbreviated to "agentive terms".

Terms of the owner, Tib. bdag po'i sgra: The name for the group of phrase linkers which, when joined to a grammatical name, show that it refers to a person or other being. There are male, female, and generic terms of the owner. The term "owner" is a direct translation of the equivalent term in Sanskrit grammar, "pati".

Terms of negation, Tib. dgag pa'i sgra: The name for the group of phrase linkers which, when placed in the appropriate position, show the negation of the meaning being shown.

The Thirty, Tib. sum bcu pa: The name of the first of eight treatises on grammar by Thumi Saṃbhoṭa that defined a grammar for the Tibetan language. Its full name is *The Root of Grammar, The Thirty Verses*.

Timing, Tib. dus skabs: The name of the one sub-division of the seventh case. See under case. It is also the name of one of the five functions of the རི་ term, in which case the Tibetan term is tshe skabs.

Transitive verb, Tib. tha dad pa'i bya tshig: Tibetan verbs are defined as being either transitive or intransitive. The definition of transitive and intransitive is very similar to that of English grammar.

Tsheg, Tib. tsheg: The name of the most frequently used of all Tibetan punctuation marks. It is a small mark with a specific shape, the size of a small dot. Its name is an onomatopoeic word equivalent to the English "snap", the sound heard when a stick, branch, or the like suddenly breaks. It is so-named because it functions literally as a break character. This fits exactly with the definition of a "break character" in typography.

Essentially speaking, it matches the use of a space in the English language to separate words. In the terminology of Tibetan grammar, it is used to separate intertshegs, *q.v.*

Verse padding, Tib. rkang skong ba'i yi ge: The name given to a letter functioning as a phrase connector which additionally is functioning to pad a line of verse so that it has the required number of intertshegs in it.

Vowel, Tib. dbyangs: The Tibetan lettering set is composed of two types of letters, no more and no less: vowels and consonants. In Tibetan language, vowels are a sound which follow the basic sound of a consonant and add a tone to it so that it is a fully-functioning letter. Therefore, the Tibetan word for vowel literally is "tone".

In Tibetan language, vowels cannot exist on their own and therefore are never written except as modifiers of a consonant. The raw sound of a vowel is obtained by starting with the ཨ་ consonant then adding the vowel to it. Vowel theory is one of the most difficult points of Tibetan grammar because the existing two of Thumi Sambhota's eight treatises which defined Tibetan grammar do not give a complete definition of the vowels. A very extensive explanation of vowels is given in volume one of the standard references to Tibetan grammar mentioned in the introduction.

Zhabkyu, Tib. zhabs skyu: The name, literally meaning "hook down at the foot", of the second of the four Tibetan vowels, having a sound simular to "u".

ABOUT THE AUTHOR, PADMA KARPO TRANSLATION COMMITTEE, AND THEIR SUPPORTS FOR STUDY

I have been encouraged over the years by all of my teachers to pass on the knowledge I have accumulated in a lifetime dedicated to study and practice, primarily in the Tibetan tradition of Buddhism. On the one hand, they have encouraged me to teach. On the other, they are concerned that, while many general books on Buddhism have been and are being published, there are few books that present the actual texts of the tradition. Therefore they, together with a number of major figures in the Buddhist book publishing world, have also encouraged me to translate and publish high quality translations of individual texts of the tradition.

My teachers always remark with great appreciation on the extraordinary amount of teaching that I have heard in this life. It allows for highly informed, accurate translations of a sort not usually seen. Briefly, I spent the 1970's studying, practising, then teaching the Gelugpa system at Chenrezig Institute, Australia, where I was a founding member and also the first Australian to be ordained as a monk in the Tibetan Buddhist tradition. In 1980, I moved to the United States to study at the feet of the Vidyādhara Chogyam Trungpa Rinpoche. I stayed in his Vajradhatu community, now called Shambhala, where I studied and practised all the Karma Kagyu, Nyingma, and Shambhala teachings being presented there and was a senior member of the Nalanda Translation Committee. After the vidyādhara's nirvana, I moved in 1992 to Nepal, where I have been continuously involved with the study, practise, translation, and teaching of the Kagyu system and especially of the Nyingma system of Great Completion. In recent years, I have spent extended times in Tibet with the greatest living Tibetan masters of Great Completion, receiving very pure transmissions of the ultimate levels of this teaching directly in Tibetan and practising them there in retreat. In that way, I have studied and practised extensively not in one Tibetan tradition as is usually done, but in three of the four Tibetan traditions—Gelug, Kagyu, and Nyingma—and also in the Theravada tradition, too.

With that as a basis, I have taken a comprehensive and long term approach to the work of translation. For any language, one first must have the lettering needed to write the language. Therefore, as a member of the Nalanda Translation Committee, I spent some years in the 1980's making Tibetan word-processing software and high-quality Tibetan fonts. After that, reliable lexical works are needed. Therefore, during the 1990's I spent some years writing the *Illuminator Tibetan-English Dictionary* and a set of treatises on Tibetan grammar, preparing a variety of key Tibetan reference works needed for the study and translation of Tibetan Buddhist texts, and giving our Tibetan software the tools needed to translate and research Tibetan texts. During this time, I also translated full-time for various Tibetan gurus and ran the Drukpa Kagyu Heritage Project—at the time the largest project in Asia for the preservation of Tibetan Buddhist texts. With the dictionaries, grammar texts, and specialized software in place, and a wealth of knowledge, I turned my attention in the year 2000 to the translation and publication of important texts of Tibetan Buddhist literature.

Padma Karpo Translation Committee (PKTC) was set up to provide a home for the translation and publication work. The committee focusses on producing books containing the best of Tibetan literature, and, especially, books that meet the needs of practitioners. At the time of writing, PKTC has published a wide range of books that, collectively, make a complete program of study for those practising Tibetan Buddhism, and especially for those interested in the higher tantras. All in all, you will find many books both free and for sale on the PKTC web-site. Most are available both as paper editions and e-books.

It would take up too much space here to present an extensive guide to our books and how they can be used as the basis for a study program. However, a guide of that sort is available on the PKTC web-site, whose address is on the copyright page of this book and we recommend that you read it to see how this book fits into the overall scheme of PKTC publications.

We have published a complete set of works on Tibetan grammar. These works are special compared to other books on the subject that have been published so far. Publications on Tibetan grammar in Western languages to date present Tibetan grammar from the perspective of Western ideas—and often incorrect ideas—about Tibetan grammar. Our publications present Tibetan grammar texts properly translated into English with extensive commentaries written on the basis of Tibetan grammar learned from the greatest Tibetan grammar experts of the author's time in classes conducted in Tibetan only and for Tibetans only.

There are two major treatises covering all the details of Tibetan grammar and with extensive explanations showing how to apply the Tibetan understanding of grammar to the Western translation of Tibetan texts. One treatise covers Thumi Saṃbhoṭa's *Thirty Verses* and the other his *Application of Gender Signs*:

- *Standard Tibetan Grammar Volume I: The Thirty Verses of Minister Thumi*, a massive treatise of several hundred pages that deals with every aspect of basic Tibetan grammar. There are long chapters on the history, revisions, and lineages of Tibetan grammar followed by authentic translations of Thumi's defining text, followed by many chapters that make clarify every aspect of the basics of Tibetan grammar. Long chapters on the cases and how they relate to English cases are included as are long chapters with thorough descriptions of every phrase linker, including ones not mentioned in *The Thirty Verses*. There are explanations of verb theory, nouns, adjectives, and other parts of speech, and punctuation.
- *Standard Tibetan Grammar Volume II: The Application of Gender Signs of Minister Thumi*, a medium-length treatise of a few hundred pages that deals with every aspect of Tibetan grammar presented in this text of Thumi. An authentic translation of Thumi's defining text is included followed by many chapters that make clarify every aspect presented in the root text. Special attention is given to the theory of transitive and intransitive verbs and how that has to be understood in order to correctly translate such Tibetan constructions into English.

Then there are a series of treatises that individually present the most common Tibetan grammar texts in use today:

- *The Great Living Tree Tibetan Grammars, Beginner's Level Tibetan Grammar Texts by Yangchen Drubpay Dorje*, the standard grammar texts currently used in all Tibetan schools as the basis for teaching Tibetan grammar together with a commentary that makes them accessible to Western readers. It is a beginner's level explanation of Thumi Saṃbhoṭa's *Thirty Verses.*
- *Tibetan Grammar: "Situ's Words", A Medium to Advanced Level Tibetan Grammar Text by Ngulchu Dharmabhadra*, the standard grammar text used to explain grammar at a medium to advanced level. It follows the system of explanation laid out in the eighth Situ Rinpoche's Great Commentary on grammar. It includes explanations of both Thumi Sambhota's *Thirty Verses* and *Application of Gender Signs* and an extensive introduction by the author.
- *Tibetan Grammar: "The Essence of Situ's Elegant Explanation", A Medium to Advanced Level Tibetan Grammar Summarizing Situ's Great Commentary*, a grammar text that presents the eighth Situ Rinpoche's complicated and difficult to follow *Great Commentary* on grammar in an easy-to-follow presentation. It includes explanations of both Thumi Sambhota's *Thirty Verses* and *Application of Gender Signs* and an extensive introduction by the author.
- *Tibetan Grammar: Application of Gender Signs Clarified, Advanced Tibetan Grammars by Yangchen Drubpay Dorje*, contains two important Tibetan texts that fully explain Thumi Saṃbhoṭa's defining grammar text called *Appli-*

> *cation of Gender Signs*. Thumi's text and these commentaries on it are difficult to understand, even for Tibetans, so the author has added extensive explanations which make the meaning easier to understand.

We make a point of including, where possible, the relevant Tibetan texts in Tibetan script in our books. We also make them available in electronic editions that can be downloaded free from our web-site, as discussed below. The Tibetan text for this book has not been included because of size constraints. However, a digital edition, together with the software needed to read it, is available on the PKTC web-site.

Digital Resources

PKTC has developed a complete range of software tools to facilitate the study and translation of Tibetan texts. For many years now, this software has been a prime resource for Tibetan Buddhist centres throughout the world, including in Tibet itself. It is available through the PKTC web-site.

The wordprocessor TibetDoc has the only complete set of tools for creating, correcting, and formatting Tibetan text according to the norms of the Tibetan language. It can also be used to make texts with mixed Tibetan and English or other languages. Extremely high quality Tibetan fonts, based on the forms of Tibetan calligraphy learned from old masters from pre-Communist Chinese Tibet, are also available. Because of their excellence, these typefaces have achieved a legendary status amongst Tibetans.

TibetDoc is used to prepare digital editions of Tibetan texts in the PKTC text input office in Asia. Tibetan texts are often corrupt so the input texts are carefully corrected prior to distribution. After that, they are made available through the PKTC web-site. These digital texts are not careless productions, but are highly reliable editions useful to non-scholars and scholars alike. All of these texts are available for free by immediate download.

The digital texts can be read, searched, and even made into an digital library using either TibetDoc or our other software, TibetD Reader. Like TibetDoc, TibetD Reader is advanced software with many capabilities made specifically to meet the needs of reading and researching Tibetan texts. PKTC software is for purchase but we make a free version of TibetD Reader available for download on the PKTC web-site.

A key feature of TibetDoc and Tibet Reader is that Tibetan terms in texts can be looked up on the spot using PKTC's digital dictionaries. PKTC has several digital dictionaries—some Tibetan-Tibetan and some Tibetan-English. Of them, the Illuminator Tibetan-English Dictionary is renowned for its completeness and accuracy. PKTC also offers a wide selection of important Tibetan reference works.

This combination of software, texts, dictionaries, and reference works that work together seamlessly has become famous over the years. It has been the basis of many, large publishing projects within the Tibetan Buddhist community around the world for over thirty years and is popular amongst all those needing to work with Tibetan language or deepen their understanding of Buddhism through Tibetan texts.

TIBETAN TEXTS

༄༅། །ཐོན་མའི་ལེགས་བཤད་སུམ་ཅུ་པའི་སྙིང་པོ་ལྗོན་པའི་དབང་པོ་བཞུགས་སོ།།

༄༅། །ན་མོ་གུ་རུ་མཉྫུ་གྷོ་ཥཱ་ཡ། །བླ་མ་མཆོག་དང་དབྱེར་མེད་པའི། །འཇམ་པའི་དབྱངས་ལ་གུས་བཏུད་ནས། །ཐོན་མིའི་ལེགས་བཤད་སུམ་ཅུ་པའི། །སྙིང་པོ་མདོར་བསྡུས་བཤད་པར་བྱ། །དབྱངས་ཀྱི་བྱ་བ་གསལ་པོ་རུ། །ཕྱེད་པ་ཨི་ཨུ་ཨེ་ཨོ་བཞི། །གསལ་བྱེད་ཀ་སོགས་སུམ་ཅུ་ཡིན། །ག་ང་ད་ན་བ་མ་འ། །ར་ལ་ས་རྣམས་རྗེས་འཇུག་བཅུ། །ད་དང་ས་གཉིས་ཡང་འཇུག་སྟེ། །ད་ནི་ན་ར་ལ་གསུམ་དང་། །ས་ནི་ག་ང་བ་མར་འཐོབ། །ག་ད་བ་མ་འ་སྔོན་འཇུག །གོ་ངོ་དོ་ནོ་བོ་མོ་འོ། །རོ་ལོ་སོ་ཏོ་སླར་བསྡུ་སྟེ། །རྫོགས་ཚིག་ཟླ་སྡུད་ཅེས་ཀྱང་བྱ། །དྲག་ཡོད་ཏོ་དང་མཐའ་མེད་འོ། །གཞན་རྣམས་མིང་མཐའི་རྗེས་མཐུན་སྦྱར། །སུ་ར་རུ་དུ་ན་ལ་ཏུ། །ལ་དོན་རྣམ་པ་བདུན་ཡིན་ཏེ། །རྣམ་དབྱེ་གཉིས་བཞི་བདུན་པ་དང་། །དེ་ཉིད་ཚེ་སྐབས་རྣམས་ལ་འཇུག །ས་སུ་ག་བ་དྲག་མཐར་ཏུ། །ང་དང་ན་མ་ར་ལ་དུ། །འ་དང་མཐའ་མེད་ར་དང་རུ། །གི་ཀྱི་གྱི་འི་ཡི་ལྔ་པོ། །རྣམ་དབྱེ་དྲུག་པ་འབྲེལ་སྒྲ་དང་། །དེ་རྣམས་ས་མཐའ་ཅན་ལྔ་ནི། །རྣམ་དབྱེ་གསུམ་པ་བྱེད་སྒྲ་སྟེ། །སྦྱོར་ཚུལ་ན་མ་ར་ལ་གྱི། །ད་བ་ས་ཀྱི་ག་ང་གི

།འ་དང་མཐའ་མེད་འི་དང་ཡི། །ཀྱང་ཡང་འང་གསུམ་རྒྱན་སྡུད་དེ། །ག་ད་བ་ས་
དྲག་མཐར་ཀྱང་། །ང་ན་མ་ར་ལ་མཐར་ཡང་། །འ་དང་མཐའ་མེད་འང་དང་
ཡང་། །ཏེ་དེ་སྟེ་གསུམ་ལྷག་བཅས་ཏེ། །ན་ར་ལ་ས་དྲག་མཐར་ཏེ། །ད་དེ་
ག་ང་བ་མ་འ། མཐའ་མེད་རྣམས་ལ་ས་སྟེ་འཐོབ། །གམ་ངམ་དམ་ནམ་བམ་
མམ་འམ། །རམ་ལམ་སམ་ཏམ་འབྱེད་སྡུད་དེ། །སྦྱོར་ཚུལ་སླར་བསྡུའི་སྐབས་
དང་མཚུངས། །ར་རུ་འི་ཡི་འང་ཡང་རྣམས། །རྐྱང་པ་མི་སྐྱོང་སྐྱོང་བའི་
ཁྱད། །འོ་འུ་འམ་གྱི་གོང་དུ་ཚོག །མེད་དང་ཡོད་པའང་དེ་བཞིན་ཡིན། །
ནས་ལས་འབྱུང་ཁུངས་དགར་སྡུད་དེ། །འབྱུང་ཁུངས་དངོས་ལ་གང་སྦྱར་
འཐུས། །རིགས་མཐུན་དགར་ནས་མི་མཐུན་ལས། །སྡུད་ལ་ནས་སྒྲ་ཕོ་ན་
འཇུག །ཀྱེ་དང་ཀྭ་ཡེ་བོད་སྒྲ་སྟེ། །ཕལ་ཆེར་མིང་གི་ཐོག་མར་སྦྱོར། །ནི་ནི་
དགར་དང་བརྣན་པའི་སྒྲ། །དང་ནི་སྡུད་འབྱེད་རྒྱུ་མཚན་དང་། །ཚེ་སྐབས་
གདམས་ངག་ལྟ་ལ་འཇུག །མིང་གི་ཐོག་མའི་དེ་སྒྲ་ནི། །ཐ་སྙད་འདས་མ་ཐག་
པ་དང་། །རྣམ་གྲངས་གཞན་ཅན་གཉིས་ལ་འཇུག །ཅི་ཇི་སུ་གང་སྤྱི་སྒྲ་སྟེ། །
ཞིག་སྟེ་སླད་འདྲ་ཕྱིར་ལ་ཅི། །སླེད་སྲིད་ལྟར་བཞིན་སྐད་ལ་ཇི། །སུ་ནི་གང་ཟག་
གང་ཀུན་ལའོ། །ན་རོ་ཡོད་མེད་པ་བ་མ། །བདག་པོའི་སྒྲ་སྟེ་ག་ད་ན། །བ་མ་
ས་དང་དྲག་མཐར་པ། །ང་འ་ར་ལ་མཐའ་མེད་ལ། །བདག་སྒྲ་ཡར་ཕྱུར་བ་དང་
ནི། །ཆ་ལ་པ་ཉིད་སྦྱོར་བ་ལེགས། །མིང་མཐའི་པ་བའང་ཕལ་ཆེར་འདྲ། །
མ་ནི་ངེས་མེད་སྐབས་དང་སྦྱར། །མ་མི་མིན་མེད་དགག་སྒྲ་སྟེ། །མ་མི་ཐོག་མ་
མིན་མེད་འཇུག །མ་ནི་བར་གྱི་གསལ་བྱེད་ལའང་། །ཚིག་ཕྲད་ཞིང་སོགས་ང་
ནམ། །འ་དང་ར་ལ་མཐའ་མེད་མཐར། །ཞིང་ཞེས་ཞེ་འོ་ཞེ་ན་ཞིག །ག་ད་བ་
དང་ད་དྲག་མཐར། །ཅིང་ཅེས་ཅེ་འོ་ཅེ་ན་ཅིག །ས་མཐའ་དམིགས་བསལ་ཞེས་
མ་གཏོགས། །ཤིང་ཤིག་ཤེ་འོ་ཤེ་ན་འཐོབ། །འོན་ཀྱང་ཁ་ཅིག་ལྷན་ཅིག་
སོགས། །མིང་གི་ཆ་དང་མ་ནོར་གཅེས། །རྐྱང་པ་འཕུལ་ལ་འ་མཐའ་
དགོས། །ཀུག་ཀྱེད་བརྩེགས་འདོགས་ཅན་ལ་སྤྱང་། །ལྷུག་པའི་དོན་མང་མིང་

མཚམས་དང་། །དོན་འབྲིང་འགྲེད་དང་དོན་ཉུང་རྫོགས། །ཚིགས་བཅད་ཀ་
མཐར་ཚིག་ཤད་བྱ། །རྫོགས་ཚིག་མཐའ་ཅན་ལྷུག་པ་དང་། །ཚིགས་བཅད་རྐང་
མཐར་ཉིས་ཤད་འཐོབ། །དོན་ཚན་ཆེན་མོ་རྫོགས་པ་དང་། །ལེའུའི་མཚམས་སུ་
བཞི་ཤད་དགོས། །ང་ཡིག་མ་གཏོགས་ཡིག་ཤད་བར། །ཚེག་མེད་དེ་སོགས་
ཞིབ་ཏུ་འབད། །ཚིག་གི།ལོ་མས་མ་བསྒྲིབས་ཞིང་། །དོན་གྱི་འབྲས་བུ་གཡུར་
ཟ་བའི། །ལེགས་བཤད་ལྷོན་པའི་དབང་པོ་འདི། །དབྱངས་ཅན་གྲུབ་པའི་རྡོ་རྗེས་
སྦྱལ།། །།

༄༅། །སུམ་ཅུ་པའི་སྙིང་པོའི་དོན་གསལ་བྱེད་ལེགས་བཤད་ལྗོན་པའི་དབང་པོ་བཞུགས་སོ།།

༄༅། །ཨོཾ་སྭསྟི། སུམ་ཅུ་པའི་སྙིང་པོའི་དོན་མདོར་བསྡུས་ནི། ~~ན་མོ་གུ་རུ་མཉྫུ་གྷོ་ཥཱ་ཡ~~ཞེས་པ་རྒྱ་གར་ལེགས་སྦྱར་གྱི་སྐད་ཡིན། དེ་བོད་སྐད་དུ་བསྒྱུར་ན་བླ་མ་འཇམ་པའི་དབྱངས་ལ་ཕྱག་འཚལ་ལོ། །ཞེས་རྒྱ་སྐད་ཀྱིས་མཆོད་པར་བརྗོད་པ་ཡིན། ~~བླ་མ་མཆོག་དང་དབྱེར་མེད་པའི། །འཇམ་པའི་དབྱངས་ལ་གུས་བཏུད་ནས།~~ །ཞེས་པ་རང་གི་བླ་མ་དང་རྗེ་བཙུན་འཇམ་པའི་དབྱངས་ངོ་བོ་དབྱེར་མེད་དུ་བལྟས་ནས་ཕྱག་འཚལ་བ་སྟེ་བོད་སྐད་ཀྱིས་མཆོད་པར་བརྗོད་པ་ཡིན། ~~ཐོན་མིའི་ལེགས་བཤད་སུམ་ཅུ་པའི། །སྙིང་པོ་མདོར་བསྡུས་བཤད་པར་བྱ།~~ །ཞེས་བློན་པོ་ཐོན་མི་སཾབྷོ་ཊའི་ལེགས་བཤད་སུམ་རྟགས་གཉིས་ནས་སུམ་ཅུ་པའི་སྙིང་པོའི་དོན་མདོར་བསྡུས་བཤད་པར་བྱ་ཞེས་བརྩམ་པར་དམ་བཅའ་བ་ཡིན། ~~དབྱངས་ཀྱི་བྱ་བ་གསལ་པོ་རྟ། །བྱེད་པ་ཨི་ཨུ་ཨེ་ཨོ་བཞི། །གསལ་བྱེད་ཀ་སོགས་སུམ་ཅུ་ཡིན།~~ །ཞེས་པ་སྤྱིར་ཡི་གེ་ལ་དབྱངས་དང་གསལ་བྱེད་གཉིས་ཡོད། དེ་ལ་མ་འདུས་པའི་ཡི་གེ་མེད། དེའི་ནང་ནས་རང་ཅག་བོད་གངས་ཅན་གྱི་སྐད་ལ་ཉེ་བར་མཁོ་བ་ཨཱ་ལི་དབྱངས་ཀྱི་བྱ་བ་གསལ་པོར་བྱེད་པའི་ཨི་ཨུ་ཨེ་ཨོ་བཞི་ཡོད། མི་གསལ་བའི་ཚུལ་དུ་ཨ་ཡང་ཡོད། ཀཱ་ལི་གསལ་བྱེད་ནི་ཀ་ནས་ཨའི་བར་སུམ་ཅུ་ཡིན། ~~ག་ང་ད་ན་བ་མ་འ། །ར་ལ་ས་རྣམས་རྗེས་འཇུག་བཅུ~~ཞེས་པ་དེ་རྣམས་མིང་གཞིའི་རྗེས་སུ་འཇུག་པས་ན་རྗེས་འཇུག་བཅུ་ཡིན་ཏེ་དཔེར་ན། ཏག ། བཟང་། བཤད། མདུན། བཏབ། བསམ། མདའ། ཤར། དཔལ། བྲུས་ལྟ་བུ། ~~ད་དང་ས་གཉིས་ཡང་འཇུག་སྟེ།~~ ཞེས་པ་ད་དང་ས་གཉིས་རྗེས་འཇུག་ཡིན་པ་མ་ཟད་རྗེས་འཇུག་གི་རྗེས་སུ་ཡང་བསྐྱར་འཇུག་པས་ན་ཡང་འཇུག་ཡིན། ~~ད་ནི་ན་ར་ལ་གསུམ་དང་།~~ ཞེས་པ་ཡང་འཇུག་ད་ནི་རྗེས་འཇུག་ན་དང་ར་དང་ལ་གསུམ་གྱི་མཐར་འཇུག་སྟེ་དཔེར་ན། ཕྱིནད། རྒྱུརད། སྐྱལད

ལྷ་བུ། ས་ནི་ག་ང་བ་མར་འཐོབ། །ཅེས་པ་ཡང་འཇུག་ས་ནི་རྗེས་འཇུག་ག་དང་
ང་དང་བ་དང་མ་རྣམས་ཀྱི་མཐར་འཇུག་སྟེ་དཔེར་ན། རྫོགས། གངས།
བཏབས། ཁམས་ལྟ་བུ། ག་ད་བ་མ་འ་སྔོན་འཇུག །ཅེས་པ་དེ་རྣམས་མིང་
གཞིའི་སྔོན་དུ་འཇུག་པས་ན་སྔོན་འཇུག་ལྟ་ཡིན་ཏེ་དཔེར་ན། གཏོར། དཔལ།
བཏབ། མཁས། འཛམ་ལྟ་བུ། གོ་ངོ་དོ་ནོ་བོ་མོ་འོ། །རོ་ལོ་སོ་ཏོ་སླར་
བསྡུ་སྟེ། །རྫོགས་ཚིག་ཟླ་སྡུད་ཅེས་ཀྱང་བྱ། །ཞེས་པ་བཅུ་གཅིག་པོ་དེ་རྣམས་ལ་
སུམ་ཅུ་པར་སླར་བསྡུ་དང་། དག་ཡིག་གཞན་ནས་རྫོགས་ཚིག་དང་། སློ་སྒོ་
མཚོན་ཅར་ཟླ་སྡུད་ཟེར། སྦྱོར་ཚུལ་ནི། དྲག་ཡོད་ཏོ་དང་མཐའ་མེད་འོ། །
ཞེས་པ་ད་དྲག་གམ་དའི་ཡང་འཇུག་ཡོད་པར་ཏོ་འཐོབ་སྟེ་དཔེར་ན། ཕྱིནད་ཏོ། །
ཀྱུརད་ཏོ། །ཙོལད་ཏོ་ལྟ་བུ། མཐའ་རྟེན་མེད་སར་འོ་འཐོབ་སྟེ་དཔེར་ན་བྱའོ་ལྟ་
བུ། གཞན་རྣམས་མིང་མཐའི་རྗེས་མཐུན་སྦྱོར། ཞེས་པ་གཞན་རྣམས་མིང་གི་
མཐར་རྗེས་འཇུག་གང་ཡོད་ཀྱང་དེ་དང་མཐུན་པར་སྦྱོར་དགོས་ཏེ་དཔེར་ན། སྡུག་
གོ །བཟང་ངོ་། །ཞིད་དོ། །བསན་ནོ། །བཏབ་བོ། །བསམ་
མོ། །མདའ་འོ། །ཤར་རོ། །གསལ་ལོ། །བྱུས་སོ། །ལྟ་བུ། སུ་
རུ་ར་དུ་ན་ལ་ཏུ། །ལ་དོན་རྣམ་པ་བདུན་ཡིན་ཏེ། །ཞེས་པ་དེ་རྣམས་ལ་ལ་དོན་གྱི་
རྣམ་དབྱེ་བདུན་ཟེར། །དེ་རྣམས་དོན་གང་ལ་འཇུག་ན། རྣམ་དབྱེ་གཉིས་བཞི་
བདུན་པ་དང་། །དེ་ཉིད་ཚེ་སྐབས་རྣམས་ལ་འཇུག །ཅེས་པ་ཤར་ཕྱོགས་སུ་འགྲོ་
ལྟ་བུ་རྣམ་དབྱེ་གཉིས་པ་ལས་སུ་བྱ་བ་དང་། ཧར་རྩྭ་བྱིན་ལྟ་བུ་རྣམ་དབྱེ་བཞི་པ་
དགོས་ཆེད་དང་། ལྷང་ཁང་དུ་རྟེན་གསུམ་ཡོད་ལྟ་བུ་རྣམ་དབྱེ་བདུན་པ་བརྟེན་
གནས་དང་། འོད་དུ་འཚེར་ལྟ་བུ་རྣམ་དབྱེ་གཉིས་པའི་ནང་ཚན་དེ་ཉིད་དང་། ཉི་
མའི་འཆར་ཁ་རུ་འགྲོ་ལྟ་བུ་རྣམ་དབྱེ་བདུན་པའི་ནང་ཚན་ཚེ་སྐབས་ཏེ་དོན་ལྔ་ལ་འཇུག
སྦྱོར་ཚུལ་ནི་ས་སུ་ཞེས་ས་མཐར་སུ་འཐོབ་པའི་དཔེ་ནི། གཡས་སུ། ལས་སུ་
ལྟ་བུ། ག་བ་དྲག་མཐར་ཏུ་འཐོབ་པའི་དཔེ་ནི། འགག་ཏུ། ལག་ཏུ།
རྒྱབ་ཏུ། འགབ་ཏུ། ཀུནད་དུ། སྐྱུརད་ཏུ་གསོལ། སྨྱལད་དུ་གསོལ་ལྟ་

བུ། ~~ང་དན་མ་ར་ཡ་ཏུ།~~ །ཞེས་པ་དྲུག་པོ་དེའི་མཐར་དུ་འཐོབ་པའི་དཔེ་ནི། སྟེང་དུ། ལྷག་དུ། མདུན་དུ། ལམ་དུ། གསེར་དུ། དཔལ་དུ་ལྟ་བུ། ~~འ་དང་མཐའ་མེད་ར་དང་ཏུ།~~ །ཞེ་པ་འ་མཐའ་རྟེན་ལ་ཡོད་པ་དང་མཐའ་རྟེན་མེད་པར་ར་དང་ཏུ་གང་རིགས་འཐོབ་པའི་དཔེ་ནི། རྟ་མདར། རྟ་མདའ་རུ། ཁར། ཁར་རུ་ལྟ་བུ། ~~གི་ཀྱི་གྱི་འི་ཡི་ལྔ་པོ། །རྣམ་དབྱེ་དྲུག་པ་འབྲེལ་སྒྲ~~ དང་། །ཞེས་པ་དེ་རྣམས་ས་མཐའ་མེད་པ་ནི། ཟངས་ཀྱི་ཞག་གླུག་ལྟ་བུ་གཞི་མཐུན་གྱི་དྲུག་པ་དང་། སྟེང་གི་མི་ལྟ་བུ་རྟེན་བརྟེན་པ་འབྲེལ་བ་དང་། ལག་པའི་སོར་མོ་ལྟ་བུ་ཡན་ལག་ཅན་དང་ཡན་ལག་འབྲེལ་བ་སོགས་རྣམ་དབྱེ་དྲུག་པ་ཚིག་སྔ་ཕྱི་འབྲེལ་བའི་སྒྲ་དང་། ~~དེ་རྣམས་ས་མཐའ་ཅན་ལྔ་ནི།~~ །རྣམ་དབྱེ་གསུམ་པ་བྱེད་སྒྲ་སྟེ། །ཞེས་པ་གི་སོགས་ས་མཐའ་ལྔ་ནི་རྣམ་དབྱེ་གང་ལ་སྦྱོར་ཡུལ་དེ་རང་གིས་ཉེ་འགྱུར་ཅི་རིགས་སུ་བྱ་བ་ཞིག་བྱེད་པའི་དོན་རྣམ་དབྱེ་གསུམ་པ་བྱེད་པ་པོའི་སྒྲ་སྟེ་དཔེར་ན་མིག་གིས་བལྟས་ལྟ་བུ་བྱ་བ་ཉེ་བར་བྱས་པ་དང་། མིག་གིས་ཤེལ་སྒྱེའི་སྒྱེ་མོ་ནས་ཕྱོགས་ཐམས་ཅད་དུ་ཡང་དང་ཡང་དུ་ལེགས་པར་བལྟས་སོ་ལྟ་བུ་བྱ་བ་འགྱུར་བར་བྱས་པའོ། །དྲུག་གསུམ་གཉིས་ཀ་སྦྱོར་ཚུལ་ནི། ~~སྦྱོར་ཚུལ་ན་མ་ར་ལ་གྱི།~~ །ཞེས་པ་དེ་རྣམས་ཀྱི་མཐར་དྲུག་གསུམ་གྱི་འཐོབ་པའི་དཔེ་ནི། མདུན་གྱི། མདུན་གྱིས་བལྟས། གཏམ་གྱི་འགོ གཏམ་གྱིས་བཤད། ཚར་གྱི་ཟེགས་མ། ཚར་གྱིས་ཆོས། ཆོས་དཔལ་གྱི་ཕྱུག ཆོས་དཔལ་གྱི་གསུངས་ལྟ་བུ། ~~ད་བ་ས་ཀྱི~~ ཞེས་པ་དེ་རྣམས་ཀྱི་མཐར་དྲུག་གསུམ་ཀྱི་འཐོབ་པའི་དཔེ་ནི། ཁྲོད་ཀྱི་གདོང་པ། ཁྲོད་ཀྱིས་བཤད། རྒྱབ་ཀྱི་གོས། རྒྱབ་ཀྱིས་ཁྱེར། གོས་ཀྱི་ཆག །གོས་ཀྱིས་གཡོགས་ལྟ་བུ་དང་། ཤུགས་ཀྱིས་གོ་དགོས་པ་ད་དྲག་ཡོད་པར་ཡང་ཀྱི་འཐོབ་པོ། ~~ག་ང་གི~~ ཞེས་པ་དེ་གཉིས་ཀྱི་མཐར་དྲུག་གསུམ་གི་འཐོབ་པའི་དཔེ་ནི། བདག་གི་ནོར། བདག་གིས་བཤད། ཚང་གི་སྣང་མ། ཚང་གིས་ར་རོ་ལྟ་བུ། ~~འ་དང་མཐའ་མེད་འི་དང་ཡི།~~ །ཞེས་པ་འ་མཐའ་རྟེན་ལ་ཡོད་པ་དང་མཐའ་རྟེན་མེད་པར་དྲུག་གསུམ་འི་དང་ཡི་གང་རིགས་འཐོབ་པའི་དཔེ་ནི།

མདའི་ལྡོང་། མདའ་ཡི་ལྡོང་། མདས་བསད། མདའ་ཡིས་བསད། ཁའི་སོ། ཁ་ཡི་སོ། ཁས་ཟས། ཁ་ཡིས་ཟས། ~~ཀྱང་ཡང་འང་གསུམ་རྒྱན་སྡུད་དེ།~~ ཞེས་པ་དེ་གསུམ་ཚིག་རྒྱན་གཉིས་དང་། སྡུད་པའི་དོན་གསུམ་ལ་འཇུག་པ་ལས་དང་པོ་ཚིག་སྔ་ཕྱི་མཐུན་པར་སྟོན་པའི་མཐུན་པའི་ཚིག་རྒྱན་ལ་འཇུག་པའི་དཔེ་ནི། མཛེས་ཀྱང་མཛེས། དྲི་མ་ཁ་ཡང་ཁ། ཤ་ཟའང་ཟ་ལྟ་བུ། ཚིག་སྔ་ཕྱི་མི་མཐུན་པར་སྟོན་པའི་མི་མཐུན་པའི་ཚིག་རྒྱན་ལ་འཇུག་པའི་དཔེ་ནི། མཛེས་ཀྱང་གོས་མེད། ཀུན་གྱི་ལྷ་ཡང་མཆོད་མཁན་མེད། རྒྱན་དགའང་ཕྱིས་བདར་མེད་ལྟ་བུ། ཀྱང་སོགས་ཀྱི་ནུས་པས་དོན་གཞན་ཞིག་སྡུད་པའི་དོན་ལ་འཇུག་པའི་དཔེ་ནི། ལྷས་ཀྱང་བཏུད་དོ། །ཤ་ཡང་ཟ། ལྟེའང་ཚིག་ལྟ་བུ། སྦྱོར་ཚུལ་ནི། ~~གདབ་ས་དྲག་མཐར་ཀྱང་།~~ །ཞེས་པ་དེ་རྣམས་ཀྱི་མཐར་ཀྱང་འཐོབ་པའི་དཔེ་ནི། བདག་ཀྱང་འགྲོ། བཤད་ཀྱང་མི་ཉན། རྒྱབ་ཀྱང་ན། ཆོས་ཀྱང་ཤེས། ཕྱིན་ཀྱང་མ་བསླེབ། བཀའ་བསྒྱུར་ཀྱང་མི་ཉན། བཀའ་སྐུལད་ཀྱང་མི་གོ་ལྟ་བུ། ~~ང་ན་མ་ར་ལ་མཐར་ཡང་།~~ །ཞེས་པ་དེ་རྣམས་ཀྱི་མཐར་ཡང་འཐོབ་པའི་དཔེ་ནི། ལྷ་ཁང་ཡང་ཡོད། ལན་ཡང་མི་འདེབ། ལམ་ཡང་ནོར། ཁར་ཡང་བཙུག །དཔལ་ཡང་ཆེ་ལྟ་བུ། ~~འ་དང་མཐའ་མེད་འང་དང་ཡང་།~~ ཞེས་པ་འ་མཐའ་རྗེན་ལ་ཡོད་པ་དང་མཐའ་རྗེན་མེད་པར་འང་དང་ཡང་གང་རིགས་འཐོབ་པའི་དཔེ་ནི། མདའང་ཤེས། མདའ་ཡང་ཤེས། སྣའི་རིང་། སྣ་ཡང་རིང་ལྟ་བུ། ~~ཏེ་དེ་སྟེ་གསུམ་ལྷག་བཅས་ཏེ།~~ ཞེས་པ་མིང་མཐའི་ཏ་རྐྱང་ཏེ་དང་། དེ་དང་། ས་སྟེ་གསུམ་མདོར་བསྡུ་ན་ཕྲུག་འཚོལ་ཏེ་བཤད། ཆོས་བཤད་དེ་གོ །སོང་སྟེ་སླེབས་ལྟ་བུ། བསྟན་བྱ་ལྟག་མ་འདྲེན་པའི་དོན་ཡིན་སྦྱོར་ཚུལ་ནི། ~~ན་ར་ལ་ས་དྲག་མཐར་ཏེ།~~ ཞེས་པ་དྲུག་པོ་དེའི་མཐར་ཏ་རྐྱང་ཏེ་འཐོབ་པའི་དཔེ་ནི། ཉན་ཏེ་གོ །འཕར་ཏེ་འགྲོ། དགྲ་བཏུལ་ཏེ་ཡོང་། རྫས་ཏེ་ཚིག །ཕྱིན་ཏེ་བསླེབས། ཆོས་བསྒྱུར་ཏེ་བཤད། སྐུལད་ཏེ་ཡི་རང་ལྟ་བུ། ~~དདེ~~ ཞེས་པ་དེའི་མཐར་དེ་འཐོབ་པའི་དཔེ་ནི། བསད་དེ་ཟ་ལྟ་བུ། ~~གང་བ་མ་འ།~~

མཐའ་མེད་རྣམས་ལ་ས་སྐྱེ་འཐོབ། །ཅེས་པ་དྲུག་པོ་དེའི་མཐར་ས་སྐྱེ་འཐོབ་པའི་དཔེ་ནི། ཀུ་བ་ཀག་སྐྱེ་བསྐྱིལ། འཕང་སྐྱེ་འཕོག །འབྲུ་བཏབ་སྐྱེ་སྐྱེས། དོན་བསམ་སྐྱེ་སྒོམ། ལུང་པའི་མདའ་སྐྱེ་གུ་ཡངས། རྡོ་སྐྱེ་ཤིན་ཏུ་སྲ་ལྟ་བུ། གམ་ངམ་དམ་ནམ་བམ་མམ་འམ། །རམ་ལམ་སམ་ཏམ་འབྱེད་སྡུད་དེ། །ཞེས་པ་གམ་སོགས་བཅུ་གཅིག་པོ་དེ་དབྱེ་གཞི་ཐོག་མར་བྱས་པའི་དབྱེ་བ་མང་པོ་འབྱེད་པའི་དོན་ལ་འཇུག་པའི་དཔེ་ནི། །བུམ་པའི་རྒྱུ་ནི་གསེར་རམ། དངུལ་ལམ། ཟངས་སམ། རག་གམ། རྫ་ལས་བྱ་འོ་ལྟ་བུ། དབྱེ་གཞི་འཇུག་ཏུ་བྱས་ནས་དབྱེ་བ་མང་པོ་སྡུད་པའི་དོན་ལ་འཇུག་པའི་དཔེ་ནི། གསེར་རམ། དངུལ་ལམ། ཟངས་སམ། རག་གམ། རྫ་ལས་བུམ་པ་བྱའོ་ལྟ་བུ། ཡང་ཡིན་ནམ་མིན། ཡོད་དམ་མེད་ལྟ་བུ་ཡིན་མིན་དང་ཡོད་མེད་ཀྱི་དབྱེ་བ་འབྱེད་པ་འབྱེད་པའི་དོན་དུ་གསུངས། དེ་རྣམས་སྦྱོར་ཚུལ་ནི། སྦྱོར་ཚུལ་སླར་བསྡུའི་སྐབས་དང་མཚུངས། །ཞེས་པ་དྲག་ཡོད་ཏམ་འཐོབ་པའི་དཔེ་ནི། ཕྱིནད་ཏམ། གྱུརད་ཏམ། སྨུལད་ཏམ་ལྟ་བུ། མཐའ་རྟེན་མེད་པར་འམ་འཐོབ་པ་ནི། ཁའམ་ལྟ་བུ། གཞན་རྣམས་མིང་མཐའི་རྗེས་མཐུན་སྦྱོར། །ཞེས་པ་མིང་མཐར་རྗེས་འཇུག་གང་ཡོད་ཀྱང་དེ་དང་མཐུན་པར་སྦྱོར་དགོས་པ་ནི། སྟག་གམ། བཟང་ངམ། ཡོད་དམ། ཡིན་ནམ། ལབ་བམ། བསམ་མམ། མཐའ་འམ། ཤར་རམ། གསལ་ལམ། བྲིས་སམ་ལྟ་བུ། ར་རུ་འི་ཡི་འང་ཡང་རྣམས། །རྐང་པ་མི་སྐོང་སྐོང་བའི་ཁྱད། །ཅེས་པ་ལ་དོན་གྱི་ར་དང་རུ། དྲུག་གསུམ་གྱི་འི་དང་ཡི། རྒྱན་སྡུད་ཀྱི་འང་དང་ཡང་རྣམས་རྐང་པ་ཁ་སྐོང་མི་དགོས་ན་ར་དང་འི་དང་འང་འཐོབ་པའི་དཔེ་ནི། རང་ཉིད་ལྷར་གསལ་ཐུགས་ཀ་ནས། །དཔལ་ལྷའི་ཕྲུག་གི་མདའ་དར་ནི། །ལྷ་མོའང་བདག་ལ་ཤིན་ཏུ་དགྱེས། །ལྟ་བུ། རྐང་པ་ཁ་སྐོང་དགོས་ན་རུ་དང་ཡི་དང་ཡང་འཐོབ་པའི་དཔེ་ནི། རང་ཉིད་ལྷ་རུ་གསལ་ནས་ནི། །ལྷ་ཡི་ཕྲུག་གི་མདའ་དར་ནི། ལྷ་ཡང་བདག་ལ་ཤིན་ཏུ་དགྱེས། །ལྟ་བུ། འོ་ཏུ་འམ་གྱི་གོང་དུ་ཚོག །མེད་དང་ཡོད་པའང་དེ་བཞིན

ཡིན། །ཞེས་པ་སླར་སྤྱིའི་འོ་དང་། མིང་གི་ཝུ་དང་། འཕྲེད་སྤྱད་ཀྱི་འམ་རྣམས་ཀང་པ་ཁ་སྐོང་མི་དགོས་ན་དེ་རྣམས་ཀྱི་གོང་དུ་ཚིག་མི་འཐོབ་པའི་དཔེ་ནི། དཔལ་ལྡན་ལྷ་མོའི་སྲུང་མའི་གཙོ། །པད་མའི་ཟེའུ་འབྲུ་དག་ལས་སྐྱེས། །བདུད་མོའམ་ཡང་ན་འབབ་མོ་སྟེ། །ལྷ་བྲུ། ཀང་པ་ཁ་སྐོང་དགོས་ན་དེ་རྣམས་ཀྱི་གོང་དུ་ཚིག་འཐོབ་པའི་དཔེ་ནི། འདི་ནི་དཔལ་ལྡན་ལྷ་མོ་འོ། །ཟེའུ་འབྲུ་ལ་བརྟེན་ཏེ་སྐྱེས། །ལྷ་འམ་ཡང་ན་བདུད་མོ་སྟེ། །ལྷ་བྲུ། ནས་ལས་འབྱུང་ཁུངས་དཀར་སྤྱད་དེ། །ཞེས་པ་ནས་དང་ལས་གཉིས་ནི་རྣམ་དབྱེ་ལྔ་པ་འབྱུང་ཁུངས་དངོས་དང་། དེའི་ཆར་གཏོགས་དཀར་གཞི་ལས་ལོགས་སུ་དཀར་བའི་དོན་དང་། མང་པོ་སྤྱད་པའི་དོན་ལ་འཇུག་པ་ལས། དེ་རྣམས་ཀྱི་དབྱེ་བ་ནི། འབྱུང་ཁུངས་དངོས་ལ་གང་སྦྱར་འཐུས། །ཞེས་པ་འབྱུང་ཁུངས་དངོས་ཡིན་ན་ནས་དང་ལས་གང་སྦྱར་ཀྱང་འཐུས་པའི་དཔེ་ནི། ས་ནས་རྩྭ་སྐྱེ། ས་ལས་རྩྭ་སྐྱེས། བ་ལས་འོ་མ་འཛོ། བ་ནས་འོ་མ་འཛོ་ལྷ་བྲུ། དཀར་བ་ལ་གཉིས། རིགས་མཐུན་དཀར་ནས་མི་མཐུན་ལས། །ཞེས་པ་དཀར་གཞི་དང་དཀར་ཆོས་རིགས་མཐུན་པ་ནས་མ་གཏོགས་ལས་མི་འཐོབ་པའི་དཔེ་ནི། ལྷ་རྣམས་ཀྱི་ནང་ནས་བརྒྱ་བྱིན་གཟུགས་མཛེས་ལྷ་བྲུ། མི་མཐུན་ལས་ཞེས་པ་དཀར་གཞི་དང་དཀར་ཆོས་རིགས་མི་མཐུན་པ་ལ་ལས་མ་གཏོགས་ནས་མི་འཐོབ་པའི་དཔེ་ནི། ལྷ་ལས་མི་དམན་ལྷ་བྲུ། སྤྱད་ལ་ནས་སྒྲ་ཁོ་ན་འཇུག །ཅེས་པ་སྤྱད་པའི་དོན་ལ་ནས་སྒྲ་ཁོ་ན་འཇུག་པ་ལས་ལ་མི་འཐོབ་པའི་དཔེ་ནི། སྤྱི་གཙུག་ནས་ཀང་མཐིལ་གྱི་བར་ལྷ་བྲུ། ཀྱེ་དང་ཀྭ་ཡེ་བོད་སྒྲ་སྟེ། ཞེས་པ་ཡུལ་ཁྱད་པར་ཅན་བོད་པ་ཀྱེ་དང་། ཡུལ་མཉམ་པ་ལ་བོད་པ་ཀྭ་ཡེ་དང་། ཞུགས་བསྟན་ཡུལ་དམན་པ་ལ་བོད་པ་ཀྭས་དང་། ཕྱ་ཡི་དང་། ཕྱས་རྣམས་ལ་འཇུག་སྦྱོར་ཚུལ་ནི། ཕལ་ཆལྟེར་མིང་གི་ཐོག་མར་སྦྱོར། །ཞེས་པ་ཕལ་ཆེ་བ་འབོད་བྱ་གང་ཡིན་གྱི་མིང་གི་ཐོག་མར་སྦྱོར་དགོས་པའི་དཔེ་ནི། ཀྱེ་རྒྱལ་པོ་ཆེན་པོ། ཀྭ་ཡེ་གྲོགས་པོ། ཀྭས་མ་ཆེན། ཕྱ་ཡེ་ཆེ་བ་དཔོན། ཕྱས་བོད་དཔོན་ལྷ་བྲུ། ཕལ་ཆེར་གྱི་ཞུགས་བསྟན་སྐབས་འགར་མིང་

གི་མཐར་སྦྱོར་དགོས་པའི་དཔེ་ནི། ངག་གི་དངོས་གྲུབ་སྐྱོལ་ཅིག་དབྱངས་ཅན་གྱི། །ལྟ་བུ། ནེ་ནེ་དཀར་དང་བསྣུན་པའི་སྒྲ། །ཞེས་པ་ནི་དཀར་གཞི་ལས་ལོགས་སུ་དཀར་བའི་དོན་དང་། ནན་ཏན་བསྣུན་པའི་དོན་གཉིས་ལ་འཇུག་པ་ལས་དང་པོ་དཀར་བའི་དཔེ་ནི། སྔོན་འགྲོ། དངོས་གཞི། མཇུག་གསུམ་ལས་དང་པོ་སྔོན་འགྲོ་ནི། ལྟ་བུ། གཉིས་པ་བརྟན་པའི་དཔེ་ནི། ཛ་ནི་བྱུང་། མར་ནི་བྱུང་། ཚྭ་ནི་བྱུང་། བུལ་ནི་བྱུང་ལྟ་བུ། སྡོམ་པ་ཐམས་ཅད་ལྡན་པར་ནི། ལྟ་བུ་ཚིག་གི་ཁ་སྐོང་རྣམས་ཀྱང་བརྟན་པའི་སྒྲར་འགྱུར་རོ། །དང་ནི་སྤྱོད་འབྱེད་རྒྱུ་མཚན་དང་། །ཚེ་སྐབས་གདམས་ངག་ལྔ་ལ་འཇུག །མིང་གི་བར་མཚམས་སུ་ཡོད་པའི་དང་ཞེས་པ་དོན་ལྔ་ལ་འཇུག་པ་ལས། དབྱེ་གཞི་མཇུག་ཏུ་ཡོད་པའི་སྤྱོད་པའི་དོན་ལ་འཇུག་པའི་དཔེ་ནི། མིག་དང་། རྣ་བ་དང་། སྣ་དང་། ལྕེ་དང་། ལུས་རྣམས་ནི་དབང་པོའོ། །ལྟ་བུ། །དབྱེ་གཞི་ཐོག་མར་ཡོད་པའི་འབྱེད་པའི་དོན་ལ་འཇུག་པའི་དཔེ་ནི། དབང་པོ་ལྔ་ནི་མིག་དང་། རྣ་བ་དང་། སྣ་དང་། ལྕེ་དང་། ལུས་པོ་ལྟ་བུ། རྒྱུ་མཚན་གྱི་དོན་ལ་འཇུག་པའི་དཔེ་ནི། ཡི་གེ་བྲིས་པ་དང་དག་བྱེད་མཁས་མིན་ཤེས་སོ། །ལྟ་བུ། དུས་བརྗོད་པ་ཚེ་སྐབས་ཀྱི་དོན་ལ་འཇུག་པའི་དཔེ་ནི། ཉི་མ་ཤར་བ་དང་འགྲོ་ལྟ་བུ། གདམས་ངག་འདོམས་པའི་དོན་ལ་འཇུག་པའི་དཔེ་ནི། ཡི་གེ་བྲིས་དང་། སུམ་རྟགས་སྦྱོང་དང་། དག་ཡིག་ཟིན་དང་ལྟ་བུ། མིང་གི་ཐོག་མའི་དེ་སྒྲ་ནི། །ཐ་སྙད་འདས་མ་ཐག་པ་དང་། །རྣམ་གྲངས་གཞན་ཅན་གཉིས་ལ་འཇུག །ཅེས་པ་མིང་གི་ཐོག་མར་ཡོད་པའི་དེ་སྒྲ་དོན་མང་པོར་འཇུག་པར་བཤད་ཀྱང་མདོར་བསྡུ་ན། ཐ་སྙད་འདས་པ་དང་། རྣམ་གྲངས་གཞན་ཅན་གཉིས་ལ་འཇུག་པ་ལས། དང་པོ་བརྗོད་ཚུལ་དེ་ཉིད་ལ་ཐད་ཀར་བཏགས་པའི་དུས་འདས་པ་ལ་འཇུག་པའི་དཔེ་ནི། མི་གཞོན་པའོ། །དེ་གཟུགས་རིང་ངོ་། །དེ་ངོ་ཞིང་ཆེའོ། །དེ་སྐད་སྨྲ་མོ་ལྟ་བུ། གཉིས་པ་དངོས་སུ་མི་གསལ་ཡང་དེ་སྒྲའི་ཤུལ་དུ་རྣམ་གྲངས་གཞན་ཞིག་སྦྱོར་རྒྱུ་ཡོད་པའི་རྣམ་གྲངས་གཞན་ཅན་ལ་འཇུག་པའི་དཔེ་ནི། དེ་ལ་ལྟོས་ཤིག །དེ་

མ་ཤོད་ཅིག །དེ་ཕྱིར་ཤོག ལྟ་བུ། ཅི་ཇི་སུ་གང་སྤྱི་སྒྲ་སྟེ། །ཞེས་པ་ཅི་
སོགས་བཞི་པོ་དེ་བྱེ་བྲག་མ་ཡིན་པར་སྤྱི་ལ་ཁྱབ་པའི་དོན་ལ་འཇུག་གོ །སྦྱོར་ཚུལ་
ནི། ཞིག་ཏེ་སླད་སྒྲ་འང་ཕྱིར་ལ་ཅི། །ཞེས་པ་ཞིག་སོགས་ལྔ་ལ་ཅི་འཇུག་པའི་
དཔེ་ནི། ཅི་ཞིག ཅི་སྟེ། ཅི་སླད། ཅི་འདྲ། ཅིའི་ཕྱིར་ལྟ་བུ་དང་།
ཞིག་ལ་ཇི་ཞིག་ལྟ་བུ་ཇི་སྦྱར་ཡང་རུང་ངོ་། །སྙེད་སྲིད་ལྟར་བཞིན་སྐད་ལ་ཇི། །
ཞེས་པ་སྙེད་སོགས་ལྔ་ལ་ཇི་འཇུག་པའི་དཔེ་ནི། ཇི་སྙེད། ཇི་སྲིད། ཇི་ལྟར།
ཇི་བཞིན། ཇི་སྐད་ལྟ་བུའོ། །སུ་ནི་གང་ཟག་ཅེས་པ་སུ་ནི་གང་ཟག་སེམས་ཡོད་
ལ་འཇུག་པའི་དཔེ་ནི། སུ་ཡིན། སུ་ཡིས་ཟེར། སུ་ལ་ཡོད་ལྟ་བུ། གང་
ཀུན་ལའོ། །ཞེས་པ་གང་ཞེས་པ་ནི་སེམས་ལྡན་སེམས་མེད་ཀུན་ལ་འཇུག་པའི་དཔེ་
ནི། གང་ནས་ཡིན། གང་ཞིག་ཡིན་ལྟ་བུ། ན་རོ་ཡོད་མེད་པ་བ་མ། །
བདག་པོའི་སྒྲ་སྟེ་ཞེས་པ་ན་རོ་ཡོད་པའི་པོ་དང་། བོ་དང་། མོ་གསུམ་དང་།
ན་རོ་མེད་པའི་པ་དང་། བ་དང་། མ་སྟེ་དྲུག་པོ་དེ་ཐུར་མིང་གི་ཆ་ཤས་སུ་མེད་
པ། རོལ་ཡས། ཀྱོལ། ཕྱུག འགག ལྷ་རྩེ། ཚང་ལྟ་བུ་ལ་
གསར་དུ་སྦྱར་ན་ཐུར་གྱི་མིང་དོན་མི་སྟོན་པར། དེའི་བདག་པོའམ། དེར་སྟོད་
མཁན་ལྟ་བུ་དོན་གཞན་ཞིག་སྟོན་པ་བདག་པོའི་སྒྲ་སྟེ་དཔེར་ན། རོལ་ཡས་པོ།
ཀྱོལ་པོ། ཕྱུག་མོ། འགག་པ། ལྷ་རྩེ་བ། ཚང་མ་ལྟ་བུ། དེ་རྣམས་
སྦྱོར་ཚུལ་ནི། གདན། བམས་དང་དྲག་མཐར་པ། །ཞེས་པ་དེ་རྣམས་ལ་
བདག་སྒྲ་པ་འཐོབ་པའི་དཔེ་ནི། གཡག་པ། བཞད་པ། ལྡན་པ། ལབ་པ།
གྲོང་གསུམ་པ། དབུས་པ། ཕར་ཕྱིནད་པ། དབང་བསྐུརད་པ། རྒྱུ་
བསྐྱིལད་པ་ལྟ་བུ། ང་འ་ར་ལ་མཐའ་མེད་ལ། །བདག་སྒྲ་ཡར་ཕྱུར་བ་དང་
ནི། །ཞེས་པ་ལྔ་པོ་དེ་རྣམས་ཀྱི་མཐའ་ཅན་གྱི་མིང་དང་སྟེབ་ས་མེད་པ་བདག་སྒྲ
ཡར་ཕྱུར་ན་བ་ཕྱེད་ཤ་འཐོབ་པའི་དཔེ་ནི། ཁ་བྱུང་བ། རྟ་མདའ་བ། བྱང་
ཤར་བ། ཁམས་རོལ་བ། གཞིས་རྩེ་བ་ལྟ་བུ། ཆ་ལ་པ་ཉིད་སྦྱོར་བ
ལེགས། །ཞེས་པ་མིང་དང་སྟེབ་ས་ཡོད་པ་བདག་སྒྲ་ཆ་ལ་སོང་ན་པ་ཉིད་སྦྱོར་བ

ཐལ་ཆེར་ལ་ལེགས་པའི་དཔེ་ནི། བྱུང་པ། མདའ་པ། གུར་པ། ངོལ་པ། རྩེ་པ་ལྟ་བུ། ~~མིང་མཐའི་པ་བའང་ཐལ་ཆེར་འདྲ།~~ །ཞེས་པ་བདག་སྒྲ་མ་ཡིན་པ་མིང་མཐའི་པ་བའང་སྦྱོར་ཚུལ་ཐལ་ཆེར་དེ་དང་འདྲ་བ། ལག་པ། རྐང་པ་ལྟ་བུ། ~~མ་ནི་ངེས་མེད་སྐབས་དང་སྦྱར།~~ །ཞེས་པ་བདག་སྒྲ་མ་ནི་འདི་ལ་འདི་འཐོབ་ཀྱི་ངེས་པ་མེད་པས་སྐབས་དང་སྦྱོར་དགོས་པའི་དཔེ་ནི། ཛམ། ཚང་མ། ཐང་མ། རོང་མ་ལྟ་བུ། ~~མ་མི་མིན་མེད་དགག་སྒྲ་སྟེ།~~ །ཞེས་པ་བཞི་པོ་དེ་སྦྱར་ན་སྦྱོར་ཡུལ་གྱི་དོན་དེ་མ་ཡིན་པའམ་མེད་པར་སྟོན་པའི་དགག་པའི་སྒྲ་ཡིན། སྦྱོར་ཚུལ་ནི། ~~མ་མི་ཐོག་མ~~ཞེས་པ་དགག་སྒྲ་མ་དང་མི་གཉིས་དགག་བྱའི་ཐོག་མར་སྦྱོར་དགོས་པའི་དཔེ་ནི། མ་ཡིན། མི་འདུག་ལྟ་བུ། ~~མིན་མེད་མཇུག~~ཅེས་པ་དགག་སྒྲ་མིན་དང་མེད་གཉིས་དགག་བྱའི་མཇུག་ཏུ་སྦྱོར་དགོས་པའི་དཔེ་ནི། ལྟ་མིན། འདྲ་མེད་ལྟ་བུ། ~~མ་ནི་བར་གྱི་གསལ་བྱེད་ཡའང་།~~ །ཞེས་པ་དགག་སྒྲ་མ་ནི་དགག་བྱའི་ཐོག་མར་སྦྱོར་དགོས་པར་མ་ཟད་དགག་བྱ་གཉིས་ཀྱི་བར་དུ་སྦྱར་ན་སྟོད་སྨད་གཉིས་ཀ་དགག་ནུས་པའི་བར་གསལ་བྱེད་ཡའང་འཇུག་པའི་དཔེ་ནི། རྟ་མ་བོང་། ར་མ་ལུག་ལྟ་བུ། ~~ཚིག་ཕྲད་ཞིང་སོགས~~ཞེས་པ་ཞིང་སོགས་དང་། ཅིང་སོགས་དང་། ཤིང་སོགས་ནི་ཚིག་དོན་སྔ་ཕྱི་ཕྲད་བྱེད་ལྟ་བུ་ཡིན། སྦྱོར་ཚུལ་ནི། ~~ང་ནམ། འ་དང་ར་ལ་མཐའ་མེད་མཐར། །ཞིང་ཞེས་ཞེའོ་ཞེ་ན་ཞིག~~ །ཅེས་པ་ང་སོགས་བདུན་པོ་དེའི་མཐར་ཞིང་སོགས་ལྟ་སྦྱོར་དགོས་པའི་དཔེ་ནི། སོང་ཞིང་། སོང་ཞེས་ཟེར་རོ། སོང་ཞེའོ། །སོང་ཞེ་ན་ལྟ་ཁང་ཞིག་ཡོད་ལྟ་བུ། དེ་བཞིན་དུ་བྲོན་ཞིང་། བསམ་ཞིང་། མི་འདའ་ཞིང་། གློར་ཤར་ཞིང་། གསལ་ཞིང་། ཞལ་ལ་ལྟ་ཞིང་ལྟ་བུ་རིགས་འདྲ། ~~གདབ་དང་དྲག་མཐར། ཅིང་ཅེས་ཅེའོ་ཅེ་ན་ཅིག~~ །ཅེས་པ་ག་ད་བ་དང་དྲག་ཡོད་པར་ཅིང་སོགས་ལྟ་སྦྱོར་དགོས་པའི་དཔེ་ནི། བཀག་ཅིང་བཀག་ཅེས་ཟེར་རོ། །བཀག་ཅེའོ། །བཀག་ཅེ་ན། རྒྱུ་ཤོག་ཅིག་ལྟ་བུ། དེ་བཞིན་དུ་བཤད་ཅིང་། བཀབ་ཅིང་། ཡིནད་ཅིང་། ཡི་གེ་བསྐུརད་ཅིང་། རྒྱ་བསྒྲིལད་ཅིང་ལྟ་བུ་རིགས་འདྲ། ~~ས་མཐར་~~

~~དམིགས་བསལ་ཞེས་མ་གཏོགས།~~ །ཞེས་པ་ས་མཐར་ཚིག་ཕྲད་དམིགས་བསལ་ཤེས་མི་སྒྱུར་བར་ཞེས་སྒྱུར་དགོས་པའི་དཔེ་ནི། ཆོས་བྱུས་ཞེས་ཟེར་རོ་ལྟ་བུ། ~~ཤིང་ཤིག་ཤེའོ་ཤེ་ན་འཐོབ།~~ །ཅེས་པ་གཞན་ས་མཐར་ཤིང་སོགས་བཞི་འཐོབ་པའི་དཔེ་ནི། བྱུས་ཤིང་། གྱིས་ཤིག བྱུས་ཤེའོ། །བྱུས་ཤེ་ན་ལྟ་བུ། གོང་གི་ཞེའོ་དང་། ཅེའོ་དང་། ཤེའོ་རྣམས་ཟེར་རོ་ཞེས་པའི་དོན་དང་། ཞེ་ན་དང་། ཅེ་ན་དང་། ཤེ་ན་རྣམས་ཟེར་ན་ཞེས་པའི་དོན་ཡིན། ~~འོན་ཀྱང་ཁ་ཅིག་ལྷན་ཅིག་སོགས། །མིང་གི་ཆ་དང་མ་ནོར་གཅེས།~~ །ཞེས་པ་འོན་ཀྱང་ཁ་ཅིག་དང་། ལྷན་ཅིག་དང་། ཆབས་ཅིག་དང་། ཐབས་ཅིག་དང་། སྟབས་ཅིག་དང་། སྐབས་ཅིག་སོགས་མིང་གི་ཆ་ཤས་ཡིན་ཅིང་ཚིག་ཕྲད་མིན་པས་དེ་འདྲ་དང་མ་ནོར་བར་བྱེད་པ་ཤིན་ཏུ་གཅེས་སོ། ~~།རྐྱང་པ་འཕུལ་ལ་འ་མཐའ་དགོས། །ཀུག་ཀྱེད་བསྐྱེགས་འདོགས་ཅན་ལ་སྦྱང་~~ཞེས་པ་ཀུག་ཅེས་པས་གི་གུ་ཞབས་ཀྱུ། ཀྱེད་ཅེས་པས་འཕྲེང་བུ་ན་རོ། བསྐྱེགས་ཞེས་པས་ར་མགོ་ལ་མགོ་ས་མགོ །འདོགས་ཞེས་པས་ཡ་ར་ལ་ཝའི་སྨད་འདོགས་བཞི་སྟེ་དེ་རྣམས་གང་ཡང་མེད་པ་ནི་རྐྱང་པ་ཡིན་ཅིང་། དེ་འདྲའི་རྐྱང་པ་ཡིན་ལ་འཕུལ་བྱེད་སྔོན་འཇུག་ལྔ་གང་ཡང་རྟུང་བ་ཡོད་ན་འ་མཐའ་ངེས་པར་དགོས་པའི་དཔེ་ནི། དཔའ་བོ། མདའ་པ། འགའ་ཞིག་ལྟ་བུ། གོང་དུ་བཤད་པའི་ཀུག་ཀྱེད་བསྐྱེགས་འདོགས་ཅན་ལ་འ་མཐའ་སྦྱོང་དགོས་པའི་དཔེ་ནི། སེམས་ཅན་གཡི། ཀྭ་པ། དར་བའི་བདེ། གོ་བྱེད་བརྡ། རྐྱང་ཏེ་ཡུ་མོ་ལྟ་བུ། ད་ནི་དབུ་ཆེན་གྱི་ཤད་དང་། དབུ་མེད་ལ་ཡང་ཐམས་ཅད་མཁྱེན་པ་ཧྐྵ་ཧྐ་དྲའི་ཕྱུག་བཞེས་སུ་ཚེག་ཤད་མཛད་པ་བཅས་ཀྱི་འཐོབ་ཚུལ་ནི། ~~ལྷུག་པའི་དོན་མང་མིང་མཚམས་དང་།~~ །ཞེས་པ་ཚིག་ལྷུག་དོན་མང་པོ་ཡོད་པར་མིང་གི་སྐད་པ་བཅད་པ་ལྟ་བུ་མ་ཡིན་པ་མིང་གི་མཚམས་སུ་ཤད་དང་ཚེག་ཤད་རེ་འཐོབ་པའི་དཔེ་ནི། རིན་པོ་ཆེའི་ཟམ་ཏོག་དང་། ངག་གི་སྒྲོལ་མ་དང་། ལི་ཤིའི་གུར་ཁང་སོགས་ལ་ལྟ་བུ། ~~དོན་འབྲིང་འབྱེད་དང་~~ཞེས་པ་དོན་མང་ཉུང་འབྲིང་ཙམ་ཡོད་ན་མིང་དོན་གྱི་དབྱེ་བ་འབྱེད་ཕྱིར་དགོས་ན་མིང་མཚམས་སུ་ཤད་རེ་འཐོབ་

པའི་དཔེ་ནི། སུམ་ཅུ་པ་དང་། རྟགས་འཇུག་གི་ལྡེ་བུ། དོན་ཆུང་རྫོགས། ཞེས་པ་དོན་ཆུང་དུ་ལས་མེད་ན་རྫོགས་མཚམས་སུ་ཤད་རེ་འབྲིབ་པ། དེ་རང་ཡིན་ལྡེ་བུ། ཚིགས་བཅད་ག་མཐར་ཚིག་ཤད་བྱ། །ཞེས་པ་ཚིག་བཅད་ཀྱི་རྐང་པའི་མཐར་ག་ཡོད་ན་ཤད་རེ་འབྲིབ་པའི་དཔེ་ནི། རྣམ་གྲངས་གཞན་ཅན་གཉིས་ལ་འཇུག །ལྡེ་བུ། རྫོགས་ཚིག་མཐའ་ཅན་ལྷུག་པ་དང་། ཞེས་པ། གོ་ངོ་དོ་ནོ་སོགས་རྫོགས་ཚིག་མཐའ་ཅན་གྱི་ཚིག་ལྷུག་ཤད་གཉིས་འབྲིབ་པའི་དཔེ་ནི། འདི་ནི་རྒྱུད་དོ། །ལྡེ་བུ། ཚིགས་བཅད་རྐང་མཐར་ཉིད་ཤད་འབྲིབ། །ཅེས་པ་རྐང་མཐར་ག་མེད་པའི་ཚིགས་བཅད་ཐམས་ཅད་ཀྱི་རྐང་མཐར་ཤད་གཉིས་འབྲིབ་པའི་དཔེ་ནི། བླ་མ་མཆོག་དང་དབྱེར་མེད་པའི། །ལྡེ་བུ། དོན་ཚན་ཆེན་མོ་རྫོགས་པ་དང་། །ཞེས་པ་དོན་ཚན་ཆེན་མོ་རྫོགས་མཚམས་ཡིན་ན་ཤད་བཞི་འབྲིབ་པའི་དཔེ་ནི། དག་བྱེད་གསལ་བའི་མེ་ལོང་རྫོགས་སོ།། །ལྡེ་བུ། ལེའུའི་མཚམས་སུ་བཞི་ཤད་དགོས། །ཞེས་པ་ལེའུའི་མཚམས་སུ་ཤད་བཞི་འབྲིབ་པའི་དཔེ་ནི། སྐུ་བལྟམས་པའི་ལེའུ་སྟེ་དང་པོའོ།། །།ལྡེ་བུ། ང་ཡིག་མ་གཏོགས་ཡིག་ཤད་དབར། ཚེག་མེད། ཅེས་པ་དབུ་ཆེན་གྱི་སྐབས་སུ་མཐའི་ང་ཡིག་དང་ཤད་ཀྱི་བར་དུ་པ་དང་ནོར་དོགས་ཀྱི་ཕྱེ་ཚེག་གམ་ང་ཚེག་འབྲིབ་པའི་དཔེ་ནི། མ་བསྒྲིབས་ཤིང་། ལྡེ་བུ། གཞན་མ་ཡི་གེ་དང་ཤད་ཀྱི་བར་དུ་ཚེག་མི་བྱེད་པའི་དཔེ་ནི། གཡུར་ཟ་བའི། ལྡེ་བུ། དེ་སོགས་ཞིབ་ཏུ་འབད། ཅེས་པ་དེ་ལ་སོགས་པ་ཚིག་དོན་ཕྲ་མོ་ལ་ཡང་ཞིབ་ཏུ་བརྟགས་ཤིང་དཔྱད་ནས་འབད་དགོས་སོ་ཞེས་པ་སྟེ། དེ་ལྟར་སུམ་ཅུ་པའི་སྙིང་པོའི་དོན་གསལ་བར་བྱེད་པ་འདི་ནི་བློ་གསར་གཞོན་ནུ་ཚིག་དོན་ཞིབ་ཅིང་རྒྱས་པ་བློའི་ར་བར་མི་ཤོང་བ་རྣམས་ཀྱི་དོན་དུ། རྩ་བ་ནས་བཤད་པའི་ཚིག་དོན་དཔེར་བརྗོད་དང་བཅས་པ་མདོར་བསྡུས་བཟུང་བདེ་བར་བྲིས་པ་ཡིན་པས། འདིའི་ཚིག་དོན་ཁོང་དུ་ཆུད་པའི་རྗེས་སུ་དེས་རིགས་འགྲེ་ནས་དཔེར་བརྗོད་མང་དུ་བྱེད་པ་དང་། སུམ་ཅུ་པའི་དོན་རྒྱས་པར་སྟོན་པའི་ལེགས་བཤད་རྣམས་ལ་ཕྲ་ཞིང་མཛངས་ལ་ཞིབ་པའི་བློ་གྲོས་ཀྱིས་ཡང་དང་ཡང་དུ་བརྟགས་ཤིང་དཔྱད་ནས་

སུམ་ཅུ་པའི་དོན་ལ་མཁས་པའི་ཕ་རོལ་ཏུ་ཕྱིན་པ་ཅི་ནས་ཀྱང་མཛད་འཚལ་ལོ། །
དགོས་མེད་ཚིག་གི་ལོ་མ་ནི། །ཕང་ཕུང་གཡོ་བས་མ་བསྒྲིབས་ཤིང་། །དགོས་
ངེས་དོན་གྱི་འབྲས་བུ་མཆོག །རོ་བརྒྱའི་བཅུད་ལྡན་གསུང་ཟ་བའི། །གསལ་
བྱེད་ལེགས་བཤད་ལྡོན་པ་འདི། །ལྡོན་པ་ཀུན་གྱི་དབང་པོ་སྐྱེ། །དབྱངས་ཅན་
གྲུབ་པའི་རྡོ་རྗེ་ཡི། །བློ་མཆོག་འཛིན་མའི་ལྷོ་ལས་འཁྲུངས། །
ཤུབྷཾ།། ༎

INDEX

1700's xvii

A Beautiful String of Pearls . . . . xvii, xviii

accounting for something else 4, 19, 46, 53

actual source 3, 17, 43, 44, 53, 66

agentive term 53

āli 8, 53, 60

āli vowels 8

Amitabha's pure land xxv

Application of Gender Signs . . . . iii, xii, xiii, xv, xxiii, xxviii, xxix, 37, 59, 74-76

arguments about grammar . xviii

bare letter 4, 24, 48, 54, 65

beginner's level texts xxviii

beginning of a name 4, 19, 46, 54

bend 4, 24, 49, 54

boundary of a name 5, 25, 49, 54

calling terms 3, 18, 44, 54

case . . vi, 2, 3, 10, 11, 16, 17, 21, 23, 26, 41, 43, 46, 47, 53-55, 59, 62, 66-68

case four 10

case linkers 59

case seven 10

case two 10

cases . . . 2, 10-12, 16, 41-43, 54, 55, 57, 58, 60, 62, 74

close of a chapter 5, 26, 49

completed lesser meanings . . 5, 25, 49

completing word . . 5, 25, 49, 55

completing words 2, 9, 40

concluder 55, 56

concluders 2, 9, 17, 40, 42

concordant class 17

concordant-class segregation 3, 17, 44, 55, 62, 66

connection . . . xv, 2-4, 9, 10, 12, 14, 16, 18, 20-23, 27, 47, 55, 67

connective term 56

consonant . 4, 22, 35, 36, 48, 54, 56, 60, 61, 66, 69

consonant letters 66

consonants . . xviii, xxii, 2, 8, 33-36, 56, 58, 60, 67, 69

continuative 42, 46, 56

continuatives 3, 14, 42

convention 4, 19, 46, 56, 59

coupled concluder 56
coupled concluders 2, 9, 40
declaration of composition . . . 8
definition of vowels and consonants xviii
dependent linker . 39, 40, 42, 44, 48, 56, 60, 61
Dharmabhadra . . vi, xiii, xx-xxii, xxvi-xxix, 24, 33, 75
differentiating tsheg . 56, 57, 62
drengbu 24, 57
eighth Situ Rinpoche xvii
ending . . . 2-5, 9-11, 13-16, 23-25, 27, 39-41, 48, 49, 57, 58, 61, 62
Essence of the Elegant Explanation . . . . iii, xxv, xxvii, xxviii
exhibitors of vowel function . . 1, 8, 33
expression of worship 7, 8
five prefixes 9, 24, 38, 57
five vowels . . . . xviii, xix, 35, 58
forceful . . . 2-4, 9, 11-16, 21, 23, 40, 41, 47, 48, 58
forceful ending 2, 9, 40, 58
forceful endings 2-4,13-15,21,47
four exhibitors of the function of the ali vowels 58
four shad 5, 26, 49
four vowels 34, 58
fronted 4, 24, 48, 58
fronting 58
Gelugpa scholars xxi
gender of the suffix letters . . . xv
Gender Signs . . . . . iii, xii, xiii, xv, xxiii, xxviii, xxix, 8, 19, 37, 58, 59, 74-76
gigu 24, 59
grammatical name . . . 31, 54, 57, 59, 61-63, 65-67
grammatical phrase . . 59, 61, 63
Great Living Tree . . . i, iii, iv, xiii, xxii-xxv, xxix, xxx, 1, 5, 7, 29, 30, 32, 34, 42, 48, 52, 57, 75
great section of meaning 5, 26, 49
Heaven of the Thirty Three xxv
highlighting 3, 18, 45, 65
hook 4, 24, 49, 59
identity 2, 10, 41, 59
immediately preceding convention 4, 19, 46, 59
include . . . x, 2, 3, 13, 15, 17, 43, 62, 65, 66
inclusion . . . 3, 13, 15-19, 42-45, 57, 59, 62, 65, 66
inclusion of multiple items . . 15
independent linker 44, 56, 60, 61
independent linkers . . 39, 44, 61
instruction . . . xxi, xxx, 3, 19, 29, 45, 51, 57
internal division of case seven 10
internal division of case two . 10
internal divisions of cases . . . 60
intransitive verb, ... 60
kāli 60
Karma Kagyu . . . vi, xvii, xxvi, 72
Khenpo Ngedon . . . . xiii, xxvii, xxviii
la equivalent 60, 61
la-equivalent 10, 43
la-equivalents 2, 10, 16, 41
linker 10, 23, 24, 31, 39-41, 43, 44, 46, 48, 49, 56, 59-63, 65, 74
linkers . xv, 4, 23, 30-32, 38-42, 44-46, 48, 51, 55, 56, 59-65, 67

Mañjughoṣha 1, 7, 8, 32, 33
medium meanings 5, 25, 49
mode of connection . 2, 3, 9, 10, 12, 14, 16, 18, 20-23
name .. v, xiv-xvi, xxiii, xxvi, xxix, 4, 5, 8, 9, 14, 18, 19, 21-25, 31, 32, 37, 40, 46-49, 53-69
names .. v, xxv, 3, 17, 18, 21, 40, 42, 44, 54-57, 60, 61, 63, 64
name-base ... 8, 9, 57, 61, 64, 66
name-bases .... xv, xvi
name's ending 2, 10, 16, 40,61,62
naro 4, 21, 24, 47, 62
Nepal ...... viii-x, xvii, xxxi, 72
Ngedon Jamyang xiii, xxvi, xxviii
Ngulchu Dharmabhadra .... vi, xiii, xx-xxii, xxvi-xxix, 33, 75
ninth century .... xiv, xvi
no ending 2-4, 9, 11, 13-15, 23, 40, 41, 48
non-case function 62
non-concordant class 17
non-concordant-class segregation 55, 62, 66
ornament 2, 13, 16, 42, 59, 62, 64
ornament and include . 2, 13, 62
ornaments 13, 64
padding . 3,16,17,19,42,45,62,68
Padma Gyaltsen ... xi, xx, xxviii
particle 62, 64
phrase linkers .. xv, 4, 23, 30-32, 48, 51, 55, 56, 60-65, 67, 68
phrase ornaments 13, 64
phrase ornaments of concordance 13, 64
phrase ornaments of non-concordance 13, 64
phrases 11, 13, 23, 32, 61, 63, 64
prefix 36, 37, 49, 57, 58, 64
prefixes .. 2, 9, 24, 37, 38, 57, 61
prior tsheg 3, 16, 42
prose 5, 25, 49, 65
Pure Letters 9, 19, 65
purges of King Langdarma . xiv
reason .. vi, 3, 19, 33, 38, 43, 45, 57, 64
renaissance of learning xvii
re-suffixes 2, 9, 37-39
Rumtek xxvi
Saṃbhoṭa ... v, xi, xii, xvi, 8, 24, 58, 59, 62, 63, 68, 74, 75
Sakya tradition .... xiii, xxi
Sanskrit ... iii, xvii, xviii, xx, xxx, 7, 27, 33, 34, 53, 60, 67, 68
Sanskrit and Tibetan grammars .... xviii, xx
second case 55, 59
segregate 3, 17, 43, 66
segregation ... 3, 17, 18, 44, 45, 55, 59, 62, 65, 66
  concordant class 17
  non-concordant class 17
segregation and of highlighting 3, 18, 45, 65
separate 3, 15, 25, 65, 68
separate and include ... 3, 15, 65
separation . 3, 15-17, 19, 42, 43, 45, 57, 59, 65
separation of multiple items . 15
seven la-equivalent cases 10
seven la-equivalents ... 2, 10, 41
seventh case 55, 68
shad .. xxiv, 5, 24-26, 49, 50, 56, 57, 66
Situ Chokyi Jungney ... xv, xvii, xx, xxiii

Situ's Great Commentary .... xi, xviii-xxi, xxvi-xxviii, 75
Situ's Words .... iii, xiii, xix, xxi, xxv-xxviii, 38, 55
sixth case 2, 11
Sonam Tsemo .... xiii, xxi
source ... xxix, 3, 17, 33, 43, 44, 53, 55, 62, 66
source, segregate, and include 3, 17, 43, 66
Speech Door Weapon 9, 66
subfix 4, 24, 49, 66
suffix .... xv, 2, 9, 10, 16, 36-41, 49, 57, 58, 61, 62, 65-67
suffixes ... xv, xvi, 2, 8, 9, 37-39, 61, 62, 65, 67
superfix 4, 24, 49, 66
ten suffix letters 37, 57, 65
ten suffixes 2, 8, 38, 39, 67
terms of calling 67
terms of connection 67
terms of generality . 4, 20, 46, 67
terms of negation .. 4, 22, 47, 68
terms of the agent 11, 67
terms of the owner . 4, 21, 47, 67
the commentaries of today iii, xvi
The Fine Explanation Great Living Tree .... iv, xxiv, 34, 57
The Great Living Tree .... i, iii, iv, xiii, xxii-xxv, xxix, 7, 29, 32, 75
the Great Living Tree grammars .... iii, xiii
The Life of Marpa xvii
the native texts of Tibetan grammar .... iii, v, vii
The Thirty ... iv, xii, xiv-xvi, xxii-xxv, 1, 2, 8, 9, 19, 27, 32-34, 36, 38, 39, 43, 46, 49, 64, 68, 74
third case 2, 11, 67
Thirty Verses .... xii, xiv, 30, 32, 33, 38, 39, 48-51, 68, 74, 75
Thonmi .... v, 8
Thorough Explanation ...... xiii, xvii, xxv, xxvii
Thumi Sambhota .. xiv, 30, 34, 39, 40, 51, 69, 75
Thumi's defining treatises .. v, x, xiii, xxii
Thumi's treatises that define Tibetan grammar iii
Tibet .. 1, i-xxvi, xxviii-xxx, 7, 8, 10, 24, 27, 29-32, 34-38, 40-42, 45, 47, 49-54, 56-66, 68, 69, 71-77, 79
Tibetan children xxii
timing 2, 3, 10, 19, 41, 45, 57, 68
transitive verb 68
transitive-intransitive verbs .. xv
tsheg 3, 5, 16, 17, 25, 26, 42, 49, 56, 57, 60, 62, 68
Tsurphu xxvi
two shad 5, 25, 26, 49
śhāstra .... xiv, xxv
verb tenses xv
verse padding 3, 16, 42, 68
vowel ... 1, 8, 33-36, 53, 54, 58, 59, 62, 69
vowel function 1, 8, 33
vowels .. xviii, xix, xxii, 8, 34, 35, 53, 56-59, 61, 69
Yangchen Drubpay Dorje .. i, iv, vi, xiii, xxi-xxiv, xxviii, xxix, 1, 5, 7, 27, 29, 30, 35, 38, 39, 42, 43, 46, 50, 52, 75
zhabkyu 24, 69
Zhey xxix

www.ingramcontent.com/pod-product-compliance
Lightning Source LLC
Chambersburg PA
CBHW031634160426
43196CB00006B/409
9789937572323